DIARIES OF A DYING MAN

William Soutar (1898-1943), was born and educated in Perth. He spent his war service with the Royal Navy from 1916 to 1919, and then went on to Edinburgh University to complete his education. Enrolled as a medical student, Soutar soon transferred to English Literature and graduated in 1923. A verse collection, *Gleanings by an Undergraduate* was published anonymously at this time.

Suffering from a progressive disease of the spine, Soutar returned to his parent's house in Perth to take up what amounted to a lifetime of private study, and by 1930 he was permanently confined to bed. He produced several volumes of poems in English in the following fourteen years, but by this time Soutar was also experimenting with Scots, and 'bairn-rhymes' in particular. His first poems in this mode were published as *Seeds in the Wind* (1933), with *Poems in Scots* in 1935 and *Riddles in Scots* in 1937. The most complete collection of his work can be found in *Poems of William Soutar: A New Selection*, ed. W. R. Aitken, Scottish Academic Press, 1988. A lively succession of friends, artists and writers came to visit Soutar in his bedroom. He recorded these events, along with his own thoughts, political views, dreams and creative processes in his diary, his journal, a dream book, a common-day book and, at the very end of his life, a record which he called 'The Diary of a Dying Man'.

This selection from Soutar's diaries and journals was made by the late Alexander Scott, Head of the Department of Scottish Literature at the University of Glasgow.

WILLIAM SOUTAR

Diaries of a Dying Man

Introduced by Alexander Scott

CANONGATE
CLASSICS
36

First published in 1954 by W. & E. Chambers. This edition, revised by W. R. Aitken. First published as a Canongate Classic in 1991 by Canongate Press Plc, 14 Frederick Street, Edinburgh.

Canongate Classics would like to thank Dr W. R. Aitken, the noted bibliographer and executor of William Soutar's literary estate, for his help in preparing this paperback edition, which has been checked against and brought into line with the original manuscripts in the National Library of Scotland.

The publishers gratefully acknowledge general subsidy from the Scottish Arts Council towards the Canongate Classics series and a specific grant towards the publication of this volume.

Set in 10pt Plantin by Falcon Typographic Art Ltd, Edinburgh & London. Printed and bound in Great Britain by Cox & Wyman, Reading, Berkshire.

British Library Cataloguing in Publication Data
Soutar, William
The diaries of a dying man
I. Title
942.082092

0 86241 347 8

Contents

Preface

When this record of courage in adversity was first published in 1954, it was received with acclaim as 'a brave and animating book' (Sir Harold Nicolson in *The Observer*). While it was recognised that one of the functions of its prose was to illuminate the remarkable range of the author's poems, it was also seen that 'its appeal should be wider, since it should be a moving experience for all who appreciate courage and magnanimity and high achievement wrested from a long struggle with pain and cramping limitations. Soutar's poetry deserves to live, but, whatever happens to it, one feels that this record of life nobly lived . . . will surely endure' (*The Weekly Scotsman*). The appearance of this new edition is sufficient proof of the truth of that perceptive prophecy.

Through his diary entries over the years, Soutar erected one of the most striking literary creations of twentieth-century Scotland, a self-portrait unrivalled in this age for insight and detail. Although his poems sought to express 'all the passion and pains of humanity stark clear from the shadows of individuality', his prose gives a day-by-day—and, at times, almost an hour-by-hour—account of his individual experience, a record that is at once idiosyncratic in subject-matter and general in relevance.

The diaries provide analyses of all the characteristic concerns of their period, the thirties and early forties—the 'social conscience', the discontent with traditional religion and the attempt to build a personal faith from the fragments of disintegrating orthodoxy, the distrust of a 'standardised' civilisation (a distrust which, in Scotland, led an increasing number to seek out and cherish what was singular in their own tradition), the debate as to the proper style for poetry, whether public or private. Yet those analyses are valuable not only in themselves but also in what they reveal of the character of the writer.

From Soutar's prose the reader can observe the process whereby a writer who began as a romantic adolescent, swithering between idealism and zany clowning, was able to transform himself into a man who could look upon the light and shade of life with pity, tenderness and humour, wringing from his own disability the advantage of a disinterestedness which was nevertheless deeply sympathetic towards human suffering. To the challenge of limitation he responded with an increased sensitivity to experience, a greater awareness of the nuances of reality, a more profound appreciation of its sorrows and its joys.

Soutar wrote many brilliant dramatic poems, and his prose contains numerous deft character-sketches, yet of all his heroes he was himself the most heroic, reacting to the constrictions of circumstances by 'an alertness ready to recognise a transitory manifestation of beauty, and to find emblems of everlastingness in familiar meetings'. The most compulsive appeal of the diaries is rooted in what he called their 'quirkiness', since 'some little aside or comment which just dropped from the pen, by the way, may prove to be a most penetrating glimpse of a situation, or a revolutionary flash lighting up some strange corner of the spirit'. Those lightning-flashes remain as vivid now as when they first illuminated the landscape of half-a-century since.

A. S. Glasgow, January 1988

Introduction

Poetry and heroism are inevitably associated with any consideration of the life of William Soutar. His poetry was the prize wrested from a battle against death and despair which he fought for half a lifetime. Death defeated him in the end, but despair never; and even of his conquest by death he made a triumph, for in that last struggle he expressed such fortitude and magnanimity as to make one proud of humankind.

Soutar's birth-place, the Scottish burgh of Perth, at the head of the estuary of the River Tay, is one of those urban areas which are fortunate enough to have both the size of a city and the spirit of a community. The town is sufficiently large to contain variety, but not so big that its individuality has been dissipated, and the surrounding countryside— only minutes distant from the centre of the burgh—is a much a part of the background of life as the streets and houses. The tidal river, too, serves to remind the townsfolk of the larger world of nature; and it was in a house not far from the river-bank, on Thursday 28th April, 1898, that William Soutar was born.

His parents came of farming stock, and his father was a craftsman, a master-joiner whose work was widely known and highly commended. Soutar himself came into the world a bouncing boy; as he writes in some unpublished humorous verses—

> In eighteen hundred and ninety-eight
> I safely passed the public gate,
> Although a monster (not in form
> But by my weight above the norm)

—explaining, in a note to these lines, 'I was a genuine twelve-and-a-half pounder. "Nurse," exclaimed the worthy Dr. McAulay: "fetch me a pinafore and we'll pack him off to school".'

The Soutar household was a religious one, his parents belonging to the Auld Licht congregation, of which the poet's father was preses for many years; as Soutar writes in an unfinished autobiographical essay, 'The religious element has coloured all my life. Brought up in a home which retained the services of grace and family worship—the Scottish Sabbath echoed for me all the week—my earliest recollection of mimicry was that of a minister. . . . A stool was my pulpit, a hand-bell rang in the invisible congregation, and some 'sugarelly' served as a humble form of wine.' But reality is apt to break in somewhat rudely upon childhood fantasies; and Soutar tells of one occasion when he had got up on a stool to [reach and 'as I was warming up finely Gran went pottering into the press and knocked the preacher right off his poopit with the press door'. This incident later served as the basis of one of Soutar's Scots poems for children—"bairn-rhymes", as he called them— *Douncome*:

> The preacher on his creepie-stool
> Was waggin airms and croun,
> When grannie wi' the press door
> Ca'd the poopit doun.

> Sic a yowlin tantrum
> And spurtlin on the flair;
> 'Loshie me!' lauched grannie,
> 'The deil's in the minister.'

Yet this early accident did not stop Soutar preaching sermons. For a sermon is an exhortation to virtue, and exhortations to virtue—to hones thought, sympathetic feeling, and responsible action—occur again and again in his later prose and verse. His vocabulary, too, was influenced by the Bible, and the movement of his verse by the

---

1. *Collected Poems*, p. 175.

rhythms of the metrical psalms. Though Soutar in his latter years subscribed to no orthodox Christian belief, his whole attitude to life—kindliness in personal relationships, concern for others, emotional and intellectual honesty—was nevertheless rooted in the religion in which he was born and bred. He loved God, and he loved his fellows; and he expressed his love both in his contacts with people and in his literary work (which, indeed, he regarded as another way of making contact with mankind).

But if Soutar loved God, he would not have been a poet had he not possessed an equally passionate appreciation of the world and the flesh. Sensuous beauty was always a delight to him; and, by one of life's ironies, that delight in sensuous beauty was first stimulated by an ostensibly religious source. One day, when he was four years old, he was left alone at his Grandmother's with 'a huge illustrated copy of *The Pilgrim's Progress*—I suddenly became aware of the beauty and allurement of the naked human body. The artist in one of his plates had engraved the nude figure of Apollyon'—and Soutar goes on to write of his 'delight in turning back again and again to the towery figure'. The fascination of physical beauty, and the fascination of spiritual grace, were to exercise an equally strong influence upon Soutar to the end of his life.

As a boy, however, he was a good deal the 'nickum'. One of his pastimes was to lean out of his Grandmother's window above the street and drop small pieces of dried earth from the window-box on the heads of passers-by; and later, at the Southern District School, he perpetrated such tricks as filling empty ink-wells with powder from fireworks and setting the whole alight. At the same school, his native spirit of independence asserted itself when, at the age of twelve, he became one of the leaders in a schoolboy strike; in the event, this 'led to the strikers being struck', but Soutar had no regrets. He was a high-spirited, active boy, captain of the football team and leader of the Seal patrol. Yet the concrete, creative imagination of the artist was already at work. As he

---

2. *Common-Day Book*, 13th June, 1939.

writes in one of his note-books, 'To me, as a boy, the Greek mythology itself was the only myth. I never questioned the reality of the god round whom the stories had been woven. These gods had been real, I thought, but had somehow passed away;' or, again, 'To youth the historic character is apt to be coloured by his mere name—thus I always associated Strongbow with the Red Indians and pictured John Knox as a very clamorous pulpit-thumper.'

Soutar began writing verse in his early teens. His first poem he remembered later as 'an "elevating" piece of eight lines or so. I forget it now, of course, but remember that one line was very like Tennyson's "stepping stones of our dead lives to higher things" idea. I would be fifteen or sixteen at the time.' By then he was a pupil at Perth Academy, where—as is the way with adolescents—he made some lifelong friendships, and where he fell in love. The girl (who grew up to marry someone else) haunted Soutar's imagination for the rest of his life; many years later, he was to realize that the reason why he preferred to see women dressed in simple dark clothes was that when he had fallen in love with X—she had been in mourning for her father; and her image moved through his dreams—of which he kept a record for some twenty years—so that he could write, 'It was strange in my dream to feel, just for a second, that same indescribable emotion pass over me which used to pass over me in those calf-love days.' During his adult life, though Soutar on occasion was physically attracted by various women, none of these evoked his passionate adoration, and at least part of the reason for this seems to have been the dominance exercised over his imagination by the figure of X—. As he was to write in his poem, *Recollection of First Love*—

> When I recall your form and face
> More than you I recall

---

3. *Dream Book*, 1st June, 1932
4. *Dream Book*, 10th April, 1925
5. *Collected Poems*, p. 261.

To come into a meeting-place
Where no leaves fall:
The years walk round this secret garth
But cannot change its guarded earth.

I have known women fonder far
Than you; more fair, more kind;
Women whose passionate faces are
Flowers in the mind:
But as a tall tree, stem on stem,
Your presence overshadows them.

They quicken from my sentient day
And stir my body's need;
But you had fixéd roots ere they
Down-dropped in seed:
They can but copy all I found
When you alone grew in this ground.

From his days at Perth Academy Soutar dated his delight in great literature, a delight which was stimulated by one of the staff, Mr. McKinlay, who taught English there for a short period after the beginning of the First World War. McKinlay, says Soutar, 'could not be called a capable teacher, for his control was lax and few paid any attention to his words', but 'somehow I sensed his keen appreciation of literature and my own interest was quickened and increased, so that I date my joy in great writing from the teaching of McKinlay.' Like Soutar himself, McKinlay was a poet—a fact which the boy discovered when some of his former schoolmaster's verse was quoted in the school magazine in an obituary notice after his death in action later in the war; twenty-five years later, Soutar could still remember one of his lines, 'As gulls that follow the mast-light.'

Soutar's last year at Perth Academy, in 1916, when he was eighteen years old, he came to regard as the most glorious of his youth. 'Now that one can look back across a fair stretch of years one is startled at the transitoriness of youth. My own, of course, was unnaturally short; and

---

6. *The Diary of a Dying Man*, 21st July, 1943.

from this distance I am aware of only one year of which I can assert—"Then I knew fully what it was to be young." That was my eighteenth year, while yet the shadow of the war was unacknowledged. Then I was one of the fleetest at the Academy: one of the strongest: first in my year at most things: I was writing poetry: I was in love: I was popular both in the class-room and on the playing field. I never reached this condition of living fulness again except in brief moments.'

But 'the shadow of the war' could not be avoided; during the same year, Soutar joined the Navy, and when the first of his diaries which remain extant begins on 8th June, 1917, he was at sea, bound for Halifax, Nova Scotia. Soutar spent two years as a sailor, serving both in the Atlantic and in the North Sea. Despite the discomfort and the danger, he enjoyed the life and came to look back upon it with a warm sense of thankfulness—'If, in the knowledge of experience, I had been confronted with the choice to forgo either my years at sea or at the University, I should have decided unhesitatingly against the latter. I should have been a trifle poorer in literary self-criticism had I never entered a University classroom. . . . Had I never been in the Navy, however, I had lost a vital contact with men and common conditions—I had been so much impoverished in life criticism . . . the actual mingling with one's ordinary and natural kind in community was a legacy to be gifted to me but once.' Soutar valued the Navy for what he experienced there of humanity; and throughout his life he continued to place more value upon human beings than upon books. Yet it shows a wonderful generosity of spirit in Soutar that he could write of his life as a sailor in this fashion, for it was during his period at sea that he contracted the illness, caused by a form of food-poisoning, which was—from one point of view—to ruin his later career.

He became ill in December, 1918, and he had spent a

---

7. *Diary*, 5th November, 1937.
8. *Journal*, 23rd January, 1940.

month in hospital before his discharge from the Navy in the following February; at the time, however, the illness was judged to be merely some form of rheumatism, and Soutar had no notion of the clouds piling up above his future when he took the train to Edinburgh in April, 1919, to become a student at the University. His first intention was to study medicine, but he found the specimens 'gruesome' and the work uninteresting—'one continual stew'—and at the end of the academic year that summer he decided to change over to the Arts faculty and read for honours in English.

At the time the chair of English was occupied by Professor Sir Herbert Grierson, the authority on Donne and metaphysical poets of the seventeenth century, and Soutar was not uninfluenced by him—'I came, in my 'Varsity years, at least three times to the Delectable Mountains: when I heard the lyrics of Donne: the Odes of Wordsworth: and Chaucer's "Pardoner's Tale".' But Soutar crossed swords with the teaching staff, too, on the subject of that remote ancestor of modern English, Anglo-Saxon, against which he wrote an attack in the undergraduate magazine. Hid neglect of the linguistic side of the degree, and his concentration upon poetry—to the almost complete exclusion of the novel— on the literary side, made it unlikely that Soutar's academic career would be crowned with the highest honours; moreover, throughout his years at the University he was dogged by ill-health, and the fact that the illness was mistakenly diagnosed as rheumatism prevented any alleviation. As he wrote, he

> walked with stiffening bones
> Among the academic stones.

In the circumstances, it was not surprising that his degree bore no relation to his intellectual capacity; he

---

9. *Diary*, 22nd April, 1919.
10. *Diary*, 3rd May, 1919.
11. *Note-Book*, 20th April, 1924.
12. *The Student*, 23rd November, 1921.

'scraped through'—to use his own phrase—with third-class honours.

In later years, Soutar looked back upon his University days with dissatisfaction; he felt that he had lived then in a narrow society and that he had worked too often for only individual ends—'in contact with minds, like my own, unawakened to social problems; and in varying measure preoccupied with studies canalized towards a career rather than broadening out into real cultural comprehensiveness—such enthusiasm and exuberance as I possessed was expended in egocentric versifying or in clowning.' And this was not merely wisdom after the event, for in a note-book of February, 1921, he had already written, 'I live in the realm of idealistic thought or in the domains of outrageous farce.' He came to regret what he considered his lack of initiative in broadening his experience of life—'I might have participated in some kind of social activity and did not . . . it is only now I realize the fitness of a co-undergraduate's advice to go into the High Street pubs and learn something of proletarian life.' At the same time, it should be said that during his four years in Edinburgh Soutar increasingly devoted himself to the study of poetry, and his first collection of verse, *Gleanings by an Undergraduate*, was published anonymously in February, 1923. While it would be an error to value the poems in this volume too highly, nevertheless they show the sensitivity of Soutar's imagination, despite the derivative nature of the verses themselves; and every poet must have the opportunity to work through his influences in order to find his own voice. The University not only introduced Soutar to those influences, but gave him that opportunity.

On the day of his graduation, 12th July, 1923, Soutar left Edinburgh by sea en route for a holiday in Orkney. But the holiday was not a success—he was ill most of the time—and when he returned to the capital in the autumn to begin

---

13. *Diary*, 30th June, 1923.
14. *Diary*, 5th July, 1940.
15. *Journal*, 23rd December, 1935.

a teacher's training course he consulted Sir John Fraser, the surgeon, as a result of which he was advised to go home to Perth to undertake a regimen of injections and massage. At first he had high hopes of recovery—as he noted in his diary during February, 1924, 'Massage. Getting along famously. Trust I'll soon be able to clear 5ft. 3ins. as in my palmy days.' But these hopes were not to be realized; on 22nd November of the same year the diary notes, 'Dr. B—called in answer to my letter. Definitely told me that my trouble was a form of spondylitis arising from irritation caused by the streptococci which had been in the bowel. Concretion between a number of the vertebrae caused by rheumatoid arthritis. Been too damned long in seeing about it.' His spine had been infected by the germ from food poisoning, and recourse to a specialist had come too late for a cure to be possible.

For the rest of his life, Soutar was debarred from any regular employment or strenuous activity. The most he could hope for was a condition of semi-invalidism whereby he might still get about and do odd jobs in the house and garden. A career as a teacher or as a journalist—the two alternatives he seems to have considered—was quite beyond his strength. Semi-invalidism was Soutar's fate for the next seven years. Yet it was during those seven years of frustration that Soutar began to 'make himself'. While he was an undergraduate, one of the teaching staff had remarked of him that 'the English honours course was not really designed for "Minor Poets, Geniuses, or Journalists". These should roam through the curricula at large'; and it was this roaming general education that Soutar now set about acquiring. He read widely in philosophy, theology, psychology, and in scientific subjects, while also extending his knowledge of the masterpieces of European literature; his personal picture of the world of ideas and the world of art was consequently greatly enlarged. And if his invalidism cut him off from the exploration of society, it presented him with the opportunity of the exploration of his own

---

16. *Diary*, 7th May, 1923.

personality, of discovering his own intellectual and emotional capabilities. He had time to think, to find out about
himself, and to decide upon his course of action.

His poetry was the medium whereby he sought to bring,
and succeeded in bringing, himself back from his solitude
'into the world again'. Not that his work during those
years enabled him to avoid every influence of frustration and despair. Sometimes, as he watched the days
of illness limp by, his comment was, 'Thus we rot into
eternity;' sometimes he referred to himself, in relation to
his parents, as 'the parasitical poet'; but, in general, the
work which he set himself, of learning as much about the
world and of expressing as much of that experience as his
condition allowed, drove away the dangers of apathy and
hopelessness.

Then, in February, 1929, he fell ill with pneumonia and,
after the lengthy confinement to bed which this involved, his
right leg became increasingly disabled. Treatment by means
of weights on the leg to counteract muscular contraction
having failed, recourse was had to surgical measures, and
in May, 1930, Soutar was operated upon so that the
adhesions on his muscles might be broken down under
anaesthetic. The present selection from his diaries begins
with his entry into the Edinburgh nursing-home where this
operation (which was unsuccessful) took place.

Soutar's diaries are extant from 1917, when he was serving in the Atlantic with the Navy, but until 1930 the entries
are usually brief notes of appointments kept and books read.
From the date of the operation, however, the entries extend
greatly, both in length and in range, until they provide a
fascinating and detailed picture of Soutar's 'still life' in the
room where he was bedfast—a life unique in achievement
as in environment. The books in which his diary was kept
belonged during this period to the *Collins Handy Diary*
series, the page measuring 4″ × 3″, with twenty lines
to the page—small dimensions, perhaps, to contain such

---

17. *Diary*, 28th February, 1928.
18. *Diary*, 1st December, 1928.

richness; but Soutar's microscopic yet finely-legibly script was able to make much of little.

The selection contained in the present volume has been made chiefly from these diaries, but for the period from January 1939, until June, 1940, I have also been able to make use of Soutar's Common-Day Book, and, for the period from 5th July, 1943, until 14th October, 1943, *The Diary of a Dying Man* which Soutar kept during those last months when he knew he was close to death. Both these volumes were written in lined exercise-books, measuring 8″ × 6″, with thirty-five lines to the page—the same type of exercise-book in which Soutar kept his manuscript poems, his *Vocable Verses* (exercises in linguistic ingenuity), his *Journal* and his record of his dreams. Since there are entries almost daily in all of these books, it is evident that Soutar, though bedfast, worked at least as hard as any writer in possession of all his physical faculties; and the content of his work proves conclusively that his devotion to life was as great as his concern with art.

For Soutar's main interest was not his own invalidism but the general human situation. Since he could not go out into the world, he brought it into his bedroom, in books, friends, children, and a multitude of acquaintances. He saw himself as a representative of mankind rather than as a solitary sufferer, and he remained 'involved in mankind' until the end. The books which led to his being declared, a month before his death, 'probably the greatest living Scottish poet', were all written during this period; and though that achievement was fundamentally based on his own character, the devoted care of his parents contributed to it more than a little—as Soutar himself acknowledged when he wrote in *The Diary of a Dying Man* on 26th September, 1943, three weeks before his death, 'I hope I shall be remembered as a poet, if for no other reason than that my folks may not be forgotten, nor the fact that they had done so much for me and had received so little in return.'

---

19. *Diary*, 28th September, 1943.

In November, 1942, Soutar became ill with pneumonia, and his recovery from this illness was slow and incomplete. On 4th July, 1943, he received official confirmation that his lungs were affected. The next day, realizing that death could not be far distant, he began writing *The Diary of a Dying Man*. It was characteristic of Soutar that during this period of increasing physical weakness his activity scarcely slackened. He saw his verse-sequence *But the Earth Abideth* through the press—it was published on 25th August; he prepared the selection of his best lyrics in English, *The Expectant Silence* (published posthumously), and set about assembling the poems in Scots which appeared in the volume of *Collected Poems* edited by his friend and fellow-makar, Hugh MacDiarmid, after his death; and he corrected the proofs of a new edition of his collection of children's poems, 'bairn-rhymes' as he called them, *Seeds in the Wind*.

William Soutar died some time between 2 a.m. and 4 a.m. on Friday, 15th October, 1943. At two o'clock he asked his mother for a glass of water and then, the night being cold, he insisted that she go to bed. When his father went in to see him two hours later, all that was mortal in the poet was at rest.

During his lifetime Soutar published nine volumes of verse, while another was privately printed in 1939, and two more were published posthumously. His best work—a high proportion of the whole—with its lyrical purity of form and potent simplicity of symbolism, expresses high courage, deep tenderness, and gusty humour. The same qualities shine from his diaries, his love of his fellows and of the common life of earth triumphing over his physical restrictions. In the course of his last fourteen years, Soutar achieved a noble magnanimity, a serenity which glows the brighter against the dark background of suffering and despair from which he wrested it.

The pages which follow are a testament to the greatest of human virtues—the courage to endure, and the courage to create. While they are not without pain—or, indeed, an occasional pettiness—the principal impression they leave on the mind is one of joyousness and grace. To make that joyousness and grace from fourteen years of restricting illness required the most delicate sensitivity and the highest resolution. William Soutar possessed both, and possessed them abundantly. It is a privilege to be associated, in however slight a way, with the continuing strength and serenity of his work.

In conclusion, I wish to express my indebtedness to Mr Douglas Young, who introduced me to Soutar's diaries; and to the poet's parents, Mr John Soutar and the late Mrs Soutar, from whom I have had every assistance, encouragement and kindness during the preparation of this selection.

Alexander Scott

CHAPTER ONE

— 1930 —

MAY

WEDNESDAY 21
D. B. Low[1] up at 11.45. Left for Edinburgh at noon. At Fraser's[2] by 3.0. After quite a brief examination said that I'd better get the leg straightened under an anœsthetic. Had had his mind made up, provisionally, before he saw me; as he had had a bed reserved for me at the Royal Scottish Nursing Home—19 Drumsheugh Gardens. Got to my room—No.18—about 4.0. To bunk. Finished reading Aldington's brochure on Lawrence. A slight thing. Odds. Wrote home. Reading. Supper. Finished reading Book I of *Golden Treasury*. Sisters and nurses here all jolly decent.

THURSDAY 22
'This is the day and this the happy morn.' At 9.30 got morphine and atropine injection. Off to theatre—*sine crepuscula toga*—at 10 a.m. Never saw actual theatre—elderly doctor chloroformed me in the 'green room'. Woke up again at 11.20 or so. Wasn't sick. Not an extra lot of reaction. Plaster of Paris troubling me more than leg—nasty knobbly part at my back—can't lie comfortably.

SATURDAY 31
Great concourse gathered to see me get splint properly adjusted, and to see me arise—'salon de orizon de crutch'. Ahem! among those present were:—Prof. Fraser: matron: assistant matron, theatre sister and my own day sister. I got up—Hooroo!!—and having clutched Fraser round the neck I wobbled about for a bit. After this skirmish have decided

to wait until Wed. before going home. I'll require some
practice, I can tell you.

JUNE

WEDNESDAY 4
Mr Fraser in—said that the leg was greatly improved. A
slight tilt in pelvis but the leg will adapt itself to that. Asked
to see more of my verse. The man's a hero. Got up at 2.30.
Dressed. Packed. Some sweat dropping around. Dad and
David arrived at 4.30. Said Good-byee to the Home. Have
had a jolly time. After much manœuvring I got wedged
into the back of the car. Home by about 8.0 after a fairly
comfortable journey. To bed at 10.30. Glad.

THURSDAY 5
Rather dud night—painful jerks in hip just as I would
become drowsy. A gnat on the borderland of sleep. Got up
at noon. Rather sore to-day—result of car-run, I suppose.
Hope I get into the walking soon and that this irritation
leaves the hip. One can neither stand nor sit in comfort.
To bunk about 8.0. Reading.

FRIDAY 6
Slept very poorly last night—leg seems to have been irritated yesterday—stayed up too long, I'm afraid. D. B. Low
looked in—said that I'd better stay in bed for the day.

SUNDAY 22
For an hour or so this evening the air was so still that not
even a leaf was moved.

WEDNESDAY 25
Up about 3.0. Left leg more painful than my dud leg now.
Must be a touch of sciatica.

JULY

FRIDAY 4
Old Mr Maconachie called. Once again I walked with him
thr' Eetaly and saw Pompey and Nappels and the catacombs

of the eternal city—how the ancient cities come to a quaint littleness as the old man mispronounces them. And so all the wealth and lasciviousness of Pompey is burnt up again in the slowly flowing lava of Mr Maconachie's mispronunciation; and the memory of that proud city becomes for me a ruined street with an old man walking upon it and peeping casually from side to side.

TUESDAY 8

Got note from Moult asking if he might include 'The Thoughts of God' among the *Best Poems of 1930*. Well! well—and who is going to be the first to come along and say—so-and-so is still to be amongst the best poems—of 2030? That's more to the point.

WEDNESDAY 16

Mr Strathern came in before 2.0 and gave me an interesting reading—here and there—from Dixon's *Hellas Revisited*. Now and again he would mouth a passage from the Greek and the Latin and our eyes would meet in wondering approval—'That's great,' we would say simultaneously—equally lost in admiration and translation.

SEPTEMBER

WEDNESDAY 10

Mr Fraser and David up at 5.40. Fraser after examination said that I'd be able to get up in a month or so. Artificial sunlight, massage and sour milk—in appropriate doses—well, whatever you say, boy.

SATURDAY 13

Folks off to talkies. 'The *Loves* of Robert Burns'—My God! My God! as if he made love so very much differently to any one else. Why not 'The Jolly Beggars' of Robert Burns—there's a better talkie for you. But Scotland hasn't any film studios—very few art studios either.

MONDAY 15

When Toke[3] and Eve[4] came back from the station they found a hedgehog on our step at the side-door. Dad brought it in on a shovel to let me see it. Wasn't very frightened like. Dark beady eyes. We left a saucer of milk for it.

TUESDAY 16
Milk all gone from saucer which we left for hedgehog—but how are we to know it was the hedgehog who enjoyed it?

OCTOBER

WEDNESDAY 1
Began reading through the *Encyclopœdia Britannica* today. Another ten years project, at least. My odyssey through Chambers' *Twentieth Cent. Dictionary* seems to be within a year of completion—that will make it nine years—one less than my calculated time.

NOVEMBER

MONDAY 3
Got prepared for getting up. D. B. Low didn't arrive—so I got up with the help of Mums and Mercer. The getting up wasn't too bad—tho' I was nearly sick, but the getting back again was a pilgrim's progress. I must have sat up too long.

SATURDAY 15
I see eight people have called this week. Counting Bowman, this means about twenty hours at least spent in mediocre conversation. My God, my God!!

SUNDAY 16
Mr Crawford, young divinity student, up—nice fellow, but what have these unexperienced undergraduates to offer to men and women. Jesus was thirty before he was ready to preach. It's a great pity that ministers do not work at something else before they turn to preaching. Then we might have not only better ministers—but fewer.

CHAPTER TWO

— 1931 —

FEBRUARY

TUESDAY 17
Finished reading *The Intimate Journals of Paul Gaugin*. Very
fresh mind—he at once joins the company of those whom
we wish we could have met. Such a distinctive French book
makes a Scot feel that he is rather a dog-collared dog. We
cannot recall Mary Stuart without seeing the shadow of
Knox at her back.

MARCH

TUESDAY 17
Scots and Irish day—but Eve never mentioned it—so I'm
afraid that the old practice is dying out. That suggests to a
facile mind that children are becoming more tolerant—or
I should say are growing up in a more tolerant atmosphere—I'm afraid, however, that the reason is apathy due
to a loss of the sense of nationality. Up wi' the banner and
let the lion learn to roar again.

APRIL

WEDNESDAY 29
Mr Mospeth along. I lay back and listened to all his plans
for the regeneration of Scotland—including one in which
he is to be editor of a terrifically high-brow and interstellar-
national review. Then he read me potential journalism of his
own and a synopsis of a short story which ought never to have
been even a synopsis—and after he had filled my room full of

cigarette smoke he 'swep out' with a smile on his face—for only a fool, and an unsympathetic fool at that, would pour cold water on schemes which are dead before they are born. Read a couple of ballads to Eve. If Scott preferred the line in his *Minstrelsy* to 'Half owre, half owre to Aberdour' I can't understand him.

JUNE

TUESDAY 2
I feel like a mindless clod these days—if only I could fall in love or experience anything else so unreasonable I might get a move on with some composition.

JULY

THURSDAY 16
Mr Maconachie called. Wonderful old man. You can note his secret pleasure now when he comes away with the phrase, 'I remember—80 years ago when I was a boy . . . ' He *must* enjoy the sound of that, for one can feel shop-soiled enough even when one can merely say 'I remember 20 years ago . . . '

FRIDAY 17
Have been in bed a year now—can't say that I worry much about it—too well looked after.

WEDNESDAY 29
An historical moment—completed my odyssey through Chambers' *Dictionary*—I began 8 years and 8 months ago. Have still 30 pages of supplement—but last night saw the completion of the dictionary proper.

AUGUST

SUNDAY 30
Finished reading *The Northern Muse*, arranged by John Buchan. A fine anthology—yet one must admit that our

greatest poems are ballads by unknown men. If a choice had to be made we could not sacrifice the ballad corpus even for Burns or Dunbar. Here are all the passions and pains of humanity stark clear from the shadow of individuality. Here are the poems of Everyman.

SEPTEMBER

WEDNESDAY 9

Nellie Buchan called. Now if a poet could work on a body as on a poem I could make Nellie into a beauty. She has the features, hair and complexion—but the eyes are rather small and her movements nervous so that her laugh is rarely musical and her smile a contortion. Ah! the dignity, the repose of Greek sculpture. I wonder if Nellie looked long enough there would she understand and find classic grace.

OCTOBER

SATURDAY 3

Finished the composition of 'The Auld Tree'[1] which I started more than two years ago—and took up again three weeks past. I am glad I waited, for during the interval the idea became more rounded and the symbolism more inevitable.

FRIDAY 30

I. D. Stewart along. Gave me a vivid résumé of Chaplin's latest film, *City Lights*. Apart from an occasional desire to leap or dance—there are two experiences which I'd like to enjoy again—a walk over Callerfountain and a Chaplin picture.

DECEMBER

TUESDAY I

Mr. Buchan along. Jawed until 9.30. I'd like to calculate how many years of one's life are spent in wobbling the tongue. Far too many, I'm sure. Ella over with Eve. Hm! but to say airy nothings to a fresh young girl—well— er—doesn't seem to be wasted time somehow. I'm afraid that philosophy is a verity only when in a vacuum.

THURSDAY 10

Mr. Robert Bain called with the MS. of 'The Auld Tree' and 7 pages of criticism. An alert little man about 65, I should say. Long white hair and a high-strung school-masterish manner. Acute critic—tho' inclined to carry his criticism into unimportant detail. His pedagogic manner firmly moulded upon his criticism—he loves to tell one what to do. He is obviously an artist *manqué*—his intuition into the processes of creation proves that. There was an air of excitement about our meeting and when Bain bade me good-bye he said 'Good morning'—tho' it was 3.30 in the afternoon. Of course I said 'Good-morning' too.

TUESDAY 15

Mr. Buchan called: a very nice man and one of the elect I am sure—yet heaven would be a very boring place if one had to be with Mr. Buchan every day—once a week is even too much—and yet he is a very likeable man—but then he is a sentimentalist, and alas! I seem to be drifting farther and farther away from the 'drop, drop slow tears' spirit. Scotland wants to forget about Barrie and the Bonnie Prince Charlie glamour for at least 50 years—and ought to turn to the stark beauty of the ballads and the courage of Knox. If a nation is to revive it ought to be fed on something more potent than wistful romanticism.

THURSDAY 17

Two pair of swanky pyjama pants came up to-day—I didn't require the jackets as I always wear a shirt, collar and tie. Why? to prove, of course, that only my lower limbs are asleep. *Nem. con.*?

CHAPTER THREE

— 1932 —

JANUARY

SATURDAY 9

Read to-day that Corot, Degas, Manet, Cézanne were all 'paternal parasites' as regards money—if I can do my share in the Scottish Renaissance perhaps I'll justify my parasitism yet. Up to yourself, my boy, it's up to yourself.

THURSDAY 14

Finished reading *Bengal Lancer* by F. Yeats-Brown. A pleasant book—by a likeable fellow. It's a pity he merely whets our appetite for a feast of yoga—but cannot satisfy it. The East has much to teach us—if we could find the true teachers. Not that we can change our western nature or would wish to change it—but placing our own culture against the eastern we can see ourselves in truer perspective. We can give something to earth which the East cannot give—but we require the East even if only as a warning of excess.

SUNDAY 17

Eve stayed in to do her Bible Questions. Due to a 'spell of cheekiness', I told her to get on with the questions by herself. At first she was going to sulk, but thought better of it and set to—with the minimum of assistance. Quite delighted with herself and vowed to do them always by herself. Thus good comes out of ill.

MONDAY 18

Eve's lesson: a headache threatening—tho' her head felt nice and cool. Accordingly I didn't suggest that she shouldn't do her piano practice—and lo! after her piano practice she was, in her own words, 'feeling a lot better'. Well, well, the strange antics of the child mind.

WEDNESDAY 27
Listened in to the Prince of Wales—on the national crisis. A very distinct speaker. What he said—as he himself admitted—was very general; indeed how could it be otherwise. Who is to solve the economic muddle? What is wrong with the modern world—as it seems to me—is its poor sense of values and the concomitant lack of a sense of proportion. So much, nowadays, panders to the lust which hopes to get something for nothing. Chance is our god.

FEBRUARY

TUESDAY 2
Mr Buchan and Miss Mackenzie got started on a religious discussion—that hobby-horse of the Scot. Arguments make me irritable these days: so much of the fuel of argumentation is merely brushwood from dead minds. In religion too—argumentation is a waste of time: you cannot argue anyone into belief—just as you cannot demonstrate that a poem is a poem: in each instance you must feel that your own experience has been illuminated and made a truth. The intellect must share in the illumination but the actual recognition of truth is not an intellectual process.

SUNDAY 21
Eve stayed in to do her Bible Questions. As she was looking through the chapter on the deception of Isaac by Jacob and the stealing of Esau's birthright—she suddenly looked up and said in a pleasantly surprised voice:—'Why, the Bible's just as good as a story book.'

MARCH

SATURDAY 12
I think that there is some truth in the assertion that a certain amount of irritability—either in body or soul—is necessary

as a ferment for creative work. If one were wholly complacent what should one desire to write about. Anyhow I have
noticed that it is often after an emotional experience arising
from a sort of accepted frustration that I find myself in a
creative mood—one may call this a desire for compensation
but that is a small part of the truth.

FRIDAY 18
Old Mr Vass toddled in at 8.0. Jawing about the Burns
country and the lesser known history of Bruce. All I had to
do was to nod the head and say Imphnm! from time to time.
I seem doomed to play the overgrown schoolboy to friendly
lecturers: and why not? Each of us has his own peculiar form
of sport and something or somebody must be the prey.

THURSDAY 24
I'm afraid these bairn-rhymes[1] which I write from time to
time must appear rather formidable for a child—yet what
can one do? Even grown-ups in Scotland are children so
far as their native tongue is concerned. All of us must wade
through the vocabulary if we are to regain our lost heritage.
If the schools were interested that would be the most fitting
field in which to sow the Word. There are signs that the
Educational Authorities are beginning to realise that Scots
is turning in its grave. Let them hurry on and dig it up.

SUNDAY 27
Martin Smith called. This man begins to get on my nerves.
As a type he is interesting—but his meanness, like a skel-
eton, seems to be thrusting itself more and more through
his skin. Judging from his hands one might say that he is
too mean to part with the filth beneath his nails. Like mean
people he prefers to sneer rather than praise; and when he
speaks his lips are opened and no more; cruel, thin lips
that move as if the teeth behind them were shut. There is
a rigidness about all his gestures as if the mean spirit denied
any generosity of movement to its body.

THURSDAY 29
Mr Buchan along—same old tales. I wouldn't have
believed (until it was 'proved on my pulses') that a
monotonous monologue could so fray one's nerves. A

fine, honest man too—but unfortunately it seems to be easier to qualify for the society of angels than for invalids. Puir God, puir God—do you ever escape the solicitations of the faithful?

APRIL

MONDAY 4
Writing and reading: continue to wrestle with words in a very sticky fashion. Perhaps my concentration on verse has made it difficult for me when I turn to prose—anyhow there is often a strained sound about such prose as I write. Of course all men, I expect, come upon these periods of mental stiffness—but they are depressing at the time and bring with them the fear that they may not pass away. At such moments if one happens upon a certain book or piece of music the mood is disintegrated—a stimulating talk with a kindred spirit may also disperse it—but alas! I rarely enjoy that. Indeed I sometimes wonder if much of the irritating tattle which is washed my way lies like a weight on the spirit.

WEDNESDAY 13
Writing and reading: To have the great masters always before one is the most thorough searchlight upon self-esteem: especially is this necessary for any Scot—since a literary reputation is so easily won here.

SUNDAY 17
Young Mr Golder —student—up for the evening. A nice young chap—but so sure, so sure. He saw Pascal's *Pensées* on my table and, tho' he hadn't read them, approved of the man because he had been told that he had found certainty. But isn't life's chief interest the fact that one is sure that one isn't sure about anything. That's an overstatement—but it will do.

TUESDAY 19
Miss Young called: being an Auld Licht and an old maid—we couldn't get past the Kirk. Now if one could walk abroad and stop to have a talk with scavengers, bargees, tramps and any chance traveller—talk might become a minor

adventure; but as I am—placed here—all talk is limited, practically, to a coterie of drably respectable minds. . . . Mr Buchan along. As usual the monologue flowed on like a backlade and I sat up like a houlat that had lost its mouse. Surely the man is beginning to see that I sink deeper and deeper into silence—if not I'll have to tell him—and some others—that one visitation a month must be the maximum. Speak about peripeteia—O! boy—I'll seem a thankless brute.

MAY

SUNDAY I
How pleasant to know that one has a couple of hours to oneself. How subtle is my form of self-flattery. What am I tacitly saying all the time to so many of my friends: 'When you leave me I shall be in much better company.'

THURSDAY I2
Now and again one cannot but feel 'his genial spirit droop'. Once or twice I have even allowed myself to echo Keats' words, 'Now . . . seems it rich to die—To cease upon the midnight with no pain'—but with a different meaning. Cowardly moments which must give place to others in which one can again quote Milton—'For who would lose tho' full of pain this intellectual being—those thoughts that wander thr' eternity:'—also with a different meaning. Keats is the more generous soul—the more human.

TUESDAY I7
How slowly one learns—and, by learning, I mean realising a truth in one's self. It is but now that I have become aware of the real nature of work. No work is real if it does not contribute to social need—either by helping in a purely utilitarian fashion or by 'entertaining'—using that word in its widest sense. There is always, for the artist, the temptation to exploit the self at the expense of society. Even great enough intellects may err here—as, I should say, Joyce is erring. Like the mastodon—the art of Joyce must ultimately become an extinct curiosity. It is not in the true line of literary evolution.

MONDAY 30

Had a shot at some verses but couldn't get going. A very strange phenomenon, this creative business. I knew what I wanted to say, and yet I couldn't have known exactly what I wanted to say or I'd have said it. There is a truth in the proverb about 'striking when the iron is hot'—when applied to creation. An idea can be hot or cold. I suppose this leads one back to the old dichotomy of the mind:—a hot idea is experienced—that is, the mind perceives it with emotion—or may one say imagination:—the cold idea is sensed by the intellect alone.

JUNE

SUNDAY 5

Broadly speaking the difference between a work of fancy and a work of imagination is this: in the former the artist escapes from mundane life by creating an ideal world of his own: in the second life is wrestled with until, like the angel, it must give its blessing—that is, until its vicissitude is charged with meaning and emotion. From another viewpoint, one might say that is the difference between imaginative childhood and manhood in an artist. Thus we find that it is usually poems of fancy which occupy the major part of anthologies for children—tho' there are many poems of imagination which the child can enjoy as a child and later can return to with the experience of manhood.

MONDAY 6

The mind is a most contrairy craitur—to-day it turns as if on ball-bearings, to-morrow the wheels are like fretting mill-stones with iron filings between them—rusty at that. But that sudden pulse of joy when you are jogging along and suddenly are lifted up as on a wave-crest of life. So with the words—those drab, peeping sparrows which, in an instant, clap their rainbow wings and soar up singing.

TUESDAY 7

Gardeners here putting in flowers in the plot of ground outside my window. Old Mr McQueen the 'boss' along supervising. It is a sad sight to watch an old man trying to keep a little plot for himself in the busy garden of the world. The strong young men are turning over the earth and he is standing as a presiding spirit—but the pose is too much for him, and soon he is sitting on a barrow and fumbling for his pipe. . . . If we dig down far enough into the mind of man I think we ought to discover that sexual shame is an attribute of fear ; and a similar fear is responsible for the cringing element in religion—fear of the 'mystery'; and this is the negative or blasphemous attitude to life, the antipole to the creative which is born of wonder.

THURSDAY 9
The artist who imagines that he is a solitary self and that his work is written merely for himself and as an expression of himself—is deceived and can never be a major artist. It is not only the innate urge which makes the artist but the sense of duty to society which drives him on. Milton's epic was written for man—and if in the writing we are presented with a private opinion also, that is but the necessary ingredient of individuality.

SUNDAY 12
Read *An Anthology of War Poems* introduced by Edmund Blunden. Owen's poetry stands well above all the others—his 'Strange Meeting' is worth all the others put together—or nearly so. Branford's sonnets are conspicuous and Sassoon's work distinctive—but Owen has not only Branford's 'high seriousness' and Sassoon's objectivity but also a sure craftsmanship—he is always the artist in full control of his medium. Beside his work Sassoon's sounds almost hysterical and Blunden's slightly artificial. After laying down this book I realised for the first time that, notwithstanding the large company of our war poets, our really fine war-poems are very few in number.

MONDAY 13
It is a great pity that critical balance is so undisciplined in Scotland—perhaps there is always a lack of critical proportion in a country with few artists; there is no contemporary corpus large enough to create a standard of judgment.

Thus—I write one poem at any length in the Doric –
and immediately *The Glasgow Herald* salutes me as a wee
Apollo—the potential saviour of the Vernacular now that
Baptist McDiarmid[2] has laid his head in the charger of
communism. In ten years it may not be so ludicrous to
mention my name alongside Hughie's—but at present it is
foolish presumption.

FRIDAY 17

Montgomerie[3] along at 5.30. A tall very thin chap—with a
most serious cast of countenance. His eyes excellent—large
and lustrous, with an open rather than ardent look. After
tea we had a long talk. I let him do most of the talking as
obviously he loves to speak of his sensations and his work.
He ought to become pretty well known in a few years.
Aetat 27, and probably as good a man as myself already.
Yet he seems to see in my work an affinity to his own latest
poetry which has sprung out of his sense of a central core
of reality in himself—the result of a 'conversion' similar
to Middleton Murry's. But I told him I had had no such
fire-baptism—and indeed I feel my nature is antipathetic
to such a 'fire baptism'. Perhaps I am learning from life in
another way.

SATURDAY 18

Now that the year is walking in all her glory—I sometimes
drop into a bitter mood. It is a season in which the body
should rejoice. The women are able to display themselves
thr' brilliant colours, and sometimes the sight of a fresh girl
with the sun in her hair seems to awaken more strongly this
year, a sense of frustration. But this is little enough—the
bitterest moments are yet to come; tho' I do not feel that
they will grow to be more than moments. There are many
different planes of battle—and many camouflages to disguise
cowardice. If I believed in a guardian angel—what ought I
to pray? 'Protect me from appealing to anybody's pity.'

MONDAY 20

How easy to become peevish in prison. Ella McQueen,
should she be in the garden, usually gives me a wave—to-day
she didn't and I felt annoyed. Silly ass.

TUESDAY 21

Today's thought:—'The union laid a gravestone upon Scottish self-hood—now the mushroom of nationality is lifting its own epitaph.' . . . Wrote a small thing in Scots—'Yesterday'. This effort isn't sentimental I trust. That is the danger when one turns to a reminiscence of childhood and 'looks back on prospects drear'. One can return so easily—the business of the poet is to look ahead. The weakness of so much of the Sitwells' poetry—at least Edith's—is just this: they dwell in a recreated childhood.

TUESDAY 28

Just realised to-day that it was round about this time, 10 years ago, when I was Mercer's⁴ age (24) that the pains and stiffness in my back began. We were on holiday at Montrose. When I look at Mercer I can scarcely accept the fact that my youth was actually dying then. Seeing him walking about in my clothes—I sometimes wonder what strange necessity brought about the humiliation of my body. Man must look for a reason and when he has lost his old gods he must peer into himself. It is not a self-compliment to surmise that one had to sacrifice one's body to make a self.

WEDNESDAY 29

Just now as I lifted my eyes to the hillside I saw the trees waving like a wall of fire. If only one could respond to life as the earth to the sun—but the heart is so often a trim little garden with neither the luxuriance nor the conflict of the jungle. It is so easy to retreat within the safe walls of mediocrity.

JULY

SUNDAY 3

Now that I drifted away from orthodoxy I cannot recollect what religion meant to me. It cannot have had a deep hold on me—because there was no agony of farewell. My most firm remembrance of any brooding on the unknown takes me back to my early boyhood—between the age of 9 and

10. Sometimes in bed I would ponder of meaning of eternity until my mind, or being, seemed to be a large whirling ball which became ever larger and larger: then when I awoke to self-consciousness, the hallucination would be gone. Otherwise, on looking back, my 'Sabbath mood' seems to have been often restless, and irritable and in incipient revolt.

WEDNESDAY 13

Have had so much trouble getting my left leg up and down that I kept it flat to-day. Spent a rotten day with it—not sharp pains; but a slow ache so that I couldn't find a position in which I could sit comfortably. . . . Often, I believe, the troubles of the mind are not so distracting to an artist as the aches of the body. Anyhow to-day, for example, I could not settle to do anything. Christopher Smart and Clare could write poetry from a mad-house—but who can write at all when suffering from influenza, say, or severe toothache?

MONDAY 25

I am truly a fellow who does not desire to be surrounded with people. I suppose that Finlayson is the only friend I would welcome as a regular weekly visitor. Apart from him I enjoy the company of one or two women—those that are free from the usual 'neighbourly' small talk. An interesting woman sharpens a man's mind—he feels that he must be at his best; especially, of course, if the woman is not only intelligent but good to look at. And underlying all is the sense of sex which gives to the companionship a spirit of adventure—in so far as any game is adventurous.

AUGUST

MONDAY 8

Bill Mackenzie up—later Jim Finlayson.[5] Bill and Jim had a lengthy argument on Russia. But what can any outsider say—any more than this: the plan seems to work—but at what human cost? Yet—our economic system isn't functioning now and at what human cost? . . . Most of the night devoted to Russia and economics—communism is in the air:

but a weekly symposium is quite enough if one is to get on with one's own job.

TUESDAY 9

The losing of the self to save it is, I suppose, the use of the self for the nation or mankind as a whole. Until the interest, of an artist, shifts from personal sensation to a sense of communal service his work cannot grow. As pure artist his work may be technically more perfect in the exploitation of the ego—but it cannot take on real greatness until it bears the burden of a people. Byron, for example, died just as he was coming fully alive. . . . Got MSS. of *Bairn Rhymes* tied together and revised. Hope this effort stirs up a little more interest. Yet we hasten slowly.

THURSDAY 11

Up to date there are but two dead men I have longed to meet—Keats and D. H. Lawrence—Lawrence especially because he speaks directly to us: he is our prophet. . . . I ought to have some work in prose on which to build when Pegasus sleeps—yet if it does not come as something which must be written, as something which only myself could make—then one is better to keep on playing at making verses: the very play is practice. . . . I think that, in some ways, slovenliness is worse than viciousness—for vice presupposes energy: a dirty saint is a paradox—a lothario must be pharisaically clean at least.

SATURDAY 13

So many of the afflicted stare into vacuity and ask why? This is folly—for the solution, if any, is to be found in the self. Even if one were justified in accusing life, one ought to realise that for man the important matter is not the suffering but how the self reacts to it. Even if he accept that the whole of the universe is but an awakening and a little noise and a gathering again into silence—man who is truly man must accept the challenge of circumstance and give it a meaning if but for a moment.

SUNDAY 14

Is it a lack of ordinary humanity in me which makes me so indifferent to people—so uncaring whether I see them again or not? Why should I expect them to bring an invigorating breath to my being—creative contact is so rare, yet one must keep the sense ever on the alert; ever stretch, as it were, a tentative tentacle in readiness to recognise a kindred spirit. Most human contact is such a drab affair, most talk but a shattering of silence—it is far more difficult to please the ear than the eye—to watch the movements of a graceful girl is more pleasurable than the hearing of wise words: the beauty of the body ought always to remind the artist that art is but the bloom on life's fruit.

FRIDAY 19

Accept your fate; but, if life has set you in a bypath, do not deceive yourself into the belief that this is the best environment for you. Life is no loving father but a force with which we must contend and to which we must adapt the self. Yet environment must not be overstressed, for if man were not the master over environment he would still be scratching a hairy hide.

SATURDAY 20

Are there many people capable of deep love? I don't suppose my worst enemy could say that I had a 'cold' nature—yet I have never had a great affection for any one. Perhaps love requires a certain amount of demonstration to keep it a lively thing: our family could be scarcely less demonstrative. Yet this deep affection of which I dream may be a romantic illusion—anyhow our family life has been very pleasant sustained by the quiet acceptance of interdependability—without any show of demonstrative endearments.

TUESDAY 23

Our happiest recollections are of moments in which we were 'possessed'—in youth this is often shown by an exuberance of physical energy and in later life by the doing of some task supremely well. For a little space we are beyond our self. Thus the finest compliment I had from my school-teachers was not any given in the class-room but one spoken on the playing fields—the North Inch. 'You were like a devil' said Mr Gow the classics master who had been watching my display of unorthodox football. Demon—or should I say—daimon-possession is not always an evil.

SUNDAY 28

Now and then a sudden, oppressive uprush of hate gathers in my chest—so that I dare not let anyone see the look in my eyes. What is the meaning of this? I believe if one could dissect such a mood to its very roots—one should find that it was hate of one's self: hatred for one's own lack of love—I have yet to prove that I am capable of love. There can be no more tragic an epitaph than that which says:—'Here lies a man who could not love.' If one had more of the herd-instinct human intercourse would be easier—but when a person comes too near me my blood instinctively cries out 'Stand back, stand back.'

MONDAY 29

I feel that I am nearing the end of a phase—some new experience, a new richness is needed in my life to bring my poetry to fullness. I suppose this means that there is something lacking in my self yet. Anyhow I feel my responsibility to life more and more—and that life demands from a man something bigger than a handful of lyrics. My life's purpose is to write poetry—but behind the poetry must be the vision of a fresh revelation for men: if one cannot help men to find bread for the body then the greater the obligation to give food for the mind. Art is for all—and the greatest art proves it.

SEPTEMBER

SATURDAY 10

Much of our Scottish verse can never hope to reach the sublime for in Scottish poetry the conversational note 'keeps breaking in'. In the Habbie stanza it would be a miracle to achieve a massive effect. Yet this same stanza is peculiarly Scottish—embodying within it so much of our northern wit and couthiness—but painfully inadequate as a medium for the stark or the sublime. Even the ballad-measure, tho' a fitting form for the expression of bare grandeur, is not able to carry a powerful imaginative conception—indeed it is not a medium for concept but for action. Its greatness is in the odd phrase.

FRIDAY 16

Very often a thought, like a moth, skims around the flame of complete consciousness for some time before it is 'illuminated by acceptance'. We are not wholly unaware of it but we do not focus on it until it has been on the margin of full consciousness for some time. Yesterday such a thought came into the flame of acceptance—namely that I cannot hope to live so long as the normally healthy man. A few have lain on their death-bed for 20 years—even granting myself so long, that means I must not look far beyond 50. It is scarcely creditable to believe that two-thirds of one's life could be gone so swiftly.

THURSDAY 29

In an intellectual period, such as our own, we are so anxious for sympathetic insight into our ideas that we tend to ignore that carnal sympathy which the body demands. Lawrence, more than any other man, has realised this need and in his insistence has incurred censures for obscenity and obsession. Yet we may learn that his fanaticism was necessary for this age which has confused reality and materialism. Despise the flesh and you distort the soul.

OCTOBER

SATURDAY 1

I love words—to look up the meaning of a word is often as pleasant as coming round a corner to behold a fresh prospect. Yet I would not forget that words are words and not windows which open on the earth—save on the unique earth as seen by a mind. A handful of earth is of more value than a word—but we require words to say so. Words have their own beauty—but they are for use and not adornment: the beauty which they have in use is the beauty which is an integral part of proper use: not an adornment—not something stuck on. . . . People look best at a distance which is far enough to allow the fancy to fill in the details which the eye must guess at. The girl that I see in the garden is not this girl to whom I speak. O! incorrigible romantic.

MONDAY 3

Fate has made it almost natural for me to accept 'the necessity of communism'—by loosening my hold from the 'property sense'. My comfort has been given to me—therefore I cannot value it in the same way as if I had won it for myself. My house is big enough if it had but one room—my estate is whatever my eyes may look on. I should miss this pleasant place if I had to leave it—but it is the loss of affectionate human contact which is true loss. A man is often solitary—but let him not pride himself upon that for no one is independent of his fellows.

TUESDAY 11

It is perfectly true that an artist acts thr' his art—thus words, paint, stone, etc., when used by the artist, are thought in action. But is such action sufficient for the whole man? At a time like this are we not forced to admit that man cannot live by the word alone—there must be the feeding of the multitude as well? Must not the artist join in the manifestation of the longed-for 'miracle': even perhaps to the detriment of his art for a season. Surely his art would awake again—reborn more potent and purged from self.

THURSDAY 13

My being must be filled with more faith and love before my work can grow to fuller expression—lyricism is not enough. I am ready to lose the self, and yet love nothing—creed or person—passionately enough. Is the fault entirely in myself—or have I not met the moment, yet. One cannot force—or rather one *must* not force the growth of the spirit: there is a bridgeless gulf between the passive and the active—to be loved and to love.

FRIDAY 21

Montgomerie up at 5.30. Tea. M. jawed on till 10.30. I read thr' most of his long poem, 'Scotland'—some fine things in it—tho' he tends to be didactic—and the freeness of the blank verse is apt to become prosy in places. M. always asking for criticism—when he is so sure of himself, why does he trouble about the opinion of others? He ought to know that he'll always be disappointed.

NOVEMBER

WEDNESDAY 2

A man's trade must stamp itself upon his mental outlook upon life—and so with the poet. The 'indefiniteness' of poetry precludes philosophy—save in the sense that from the mood and the moment may awake a philosophical aura peculiar to the momentary experience. Poetry cannot be fixed—but is, as life, fluid—the same yet different like the arch of a waterfall. And so the poet's religion and philosophy is not a system but a recognition of things as they are—he cannot be didactic for the application of a moral upon nature is a personal predilection and he would rather speak for all than speak but for himself.

THURSDAY 10

For some weeks past I have found myself, from time to time, putting out an imaginary hand as if to touch the earth in a comprehensive gesture of love—but I do not deceive myself by these vague stirrings of affection: it is so easy to love a 'thing': one must learn to love people first.

THURSDAY 17

It is easier to pile up arguments to support the status quo than to prove the rightness of change—for change demands faith, and the first steps must be into the unknown. If a man is determined to wait until he is assured of the rightness of his faith—then he must be content to rot in stagnation. . . . Odd writing—but merely 'odds'—more and more am I waiting to be filled with faith: more and more I realise the necessity of service—am I blind; is my heart a stone—what lack I yet?

DECEMBER

FRIDAY 2

Why it is so important for a poet at a national crisis, such as our own to-day, to have a creative faith is due to the fact that he alone can clothe his faith in symbols which stir the depths of the racial consciousness. No one can argue another into a faith—nor can poetry force faith upon a people, but it can sensitise the national spirit to the need of the hour—poets if they be men of faith can make it easier for others to look abroad and see the truth. And thus it is that I am no longer contented with a vague faith in life: the moment demands a more directional functioning: perhaps it is a challenge to the poets to come down from Parnassus for a season.

SATURDAY 3

We aren't a family who indulge much in tittle-tattle—but even from such private symposiums as we *do* occasionally indulge in I can gather how petty, vindictive and uncharitable must be the conversation in many homes. How hypocritical we all can be and are—bowing, smiling, shaking the hand, kissing the cheek, offering the gift—and anon dissecting the same friend or acquaintance to lay bare the ultimate lily-livered drop of inhumanity that is in him. The clannishness of the family, if responsible for so much social stability, is yet very often a thorn of selfishness in the body of brotherliness. What if we all would confess our secret thoughts and sayings? Alas how many of us are human enough to welcome the truth.

THURSDAY 8

I believe it would be a good thing for the majority of Christians if they hid their Bibles away for a number of years—then returned to the words of Jesus with, let us hope, the cobwebs of custom blown from them. It is a pity that so few, if any, come on the Bible naturally—as a heaven-sent gift, like a flower. Alas! it is so pawed upon by those who hand it to us that we miss the freshness. What, in the end, are the most important books in a man's life—but those upon which he has stumbled himself: they become personal to him in a way all 'recommended books' can never rival.

SATURDAY 10

In our early religious myth the ideal condition of man was gardening and poetry—for Adam was a poet fitting names to things. Perhaps there is a fundamental significance about this relationship of earth-companionship and poetry—and it is unnatural for a maker of words to be merely a maker of words—or that and some sort of clean-collared worker.

Poets ought to keep close to earth for their most insinuous temptation is to get into the clouds where they lose themselves in an ideal world. And what is true for the poet is true for youth—when it is possible for everyman to be a potential poet—merely intellectual work is apt to unbalance the selfhood. All should be men of handicraft.

TUESDAY 13
The poet must retain a certain childish impressibility—he cannot escape even if he would. Thus I find myself, all of a sudden, bursting out into song or laughter; or aware of a surly core of ill-temper festering inside me like a ferment. And now that Christmas bells are within hearing I sense a modicum at least of that suppressed excitement which is already bubbling up in the child.

TUESDAY 20
Nietzsche is one of the very few philosophers who remain poets in the midst of their philosophising; perhaps he is the only one. His words are often as near to actual living as it is possible for words to be—they are very nearly made flesh. Often, when reading Nietzsche, one feels as if one were on a high hill in a bright windy day; we are always aware of action, space and an atmosphere which is best rendered by the word 'caller'. We may call Nietzsche's philosophy pantomimic—every word is a bold gesture, a moment in a noble dance.

CHAPTER FOUR

— 1933 —

JANUARY

SUNDAY I
Martin Smith up after dinner. Brought me a box of 'bines
which I could scarcely accept without a blush after my odd
remarks on his parsimony, 'Ah! gently scan your brother
man.'

TUESDAY 10
For some time past I have been growing towards a realisation
of the generosity of life—and that it is this lively generous-
ness which is exemplified in great men and women: the seal
which distinguishes them. No finer symbol of this has come
my way than that of Isadora Duncan dancing with breasts so
full of milk that they overflowed—the rich, natural freedom
of this woman's life, its very waywardness, is like a flower in
the waste land of the machines. . . . What is love but that
generous receptiveness and recreation mentioned above.

When I grow in *this* grace then I shall give back to life
something of that richness which life has given to me. I can
but blame some fatal flaw in my self's self for the humiliation
of a fine body.

WEDNESDAY 11
Living in so comfortable a cell as my own leaves little cause
for complaint—yet to bring the world picture into it I should
have a second window from which I could look out on the
sea: and near enough also for me to hear it.

FRIDAY 13
The blood is older than the self. So it would seem; for
suddenly we can feel that our greatest need is to have a

woman in our arms—tho' in another moment we realise
how fleeting the desire and how frustrate were its fulfilment without love. Yet the flooding impulse wells up from
the deeps and for a space all other desires are drowned
under it.

FRIDAY 27

I wonder if fit mortals realise that infirmity makes the
most ordinary actions wonderful. A person, like myself,
set aside from the thoroughfare of life can often look on life's
manifestation with a detachment denied the protagonist
in the market-place. Common acts become isolated from
particular times and places and grow, by recollection, into
moments of beauty loved in themselves without desire or
regret. Thus everyday phrases can bring to such a watcher
a rounded image of loveliness mysteriously coloured by the
consciousness that he himself can no longer enact them;
phrases such as 'he lifted a stone', 'he stood by the sea',
'he walked into the wood'.

SATURDAY 28

The men who are to prepare the people for any 'brave
new world' are to be men who fully realise that many
of the common people are in no wise eager for change
—especially a change in themselves. It is sentimentality
to blind ourselves to the fact that many human beings
are content to remain in pleasurable content. The artist
especially must not forget this. Accordingly, the art which
is to move the people towards a renaissance must be simple
in the sense that all the basic truths of life are simple—the
symbols fitting the comprehension of men whose lives are
ever near reality—metaphors, that is, which grow out of
the experience of humble folk and their daily toil: in short
parables after the fashion of the gospel.

FEBRUARY

FRIDAY 24

When the life of the flesh is thwarted at a time when the
body should be most alive—then one, such as myself,

must guard against setting a disproportionate value upon the body. The praise of earth which has been an ever more insistent theme in my verse is honest; but without due care it might become fanatical—unbalanced by the frustration of my own flesh. Nor is the increased sensitivity to nature and human grace, born of bodily imparticipation, without its tendency towards mere sensuality wherein passion becomes a subterfuge of hate.

SUNDAY 26

I believe that our age is waiting for a great satirist—one able to survey the multifarious manifestations of folly and hate and, with surety, thrust the scalpel of his creative wit sheer into the central cancer of our social deathliness from which all the lesser causes of corruption proliferate. Surely there has never been a period in the world's history so prolific in rational lunacy and social chaos; when the man with the godlike eye looks abroad his devastating laughter will be more terrible than any righteous wrath.

MONDAY 27

Joy comes in those moments, preceding actual creation, when the water of life seems to permeate the pool of one's personality—the heart is physically sensible of it as if a warm hand were under it lifting it with gentle exultation as the blood beats. It is a momentary knowledge of a love which is beyond personality and the conflicting passions of personal affection. Without it art is an intellectual exercise or the embodiment of day-dream—cold or fantastical, barren or moonstruck, finicky or emasculate.

MARCH

FRIDAY 17

Neil Gunn[1] called. I knew him at once, of course, from his photographs. A bit older looking than I had imagined. He has a fine strong face—better in profile as his eyes are apt to wander into a sort of cast. A fluent and convincing talker—an honest talker. He seems a much more potent man than his books suggest. He has the certainty which

Grieve lacks—and yet lacks the wonder of Grieve. With
Grieve we can indulge and escape—with Gunn we must
face our weaknesses and strive to be better men. Grieve is
the more gifted but Gunn by doing well what he can do may
yet achieve more.

APRIL

WEDNESDAY 5

How small an impetus may start a 'train' of thought. The
other day, in a drifted moment, I found that by rubbing the
one hand against the other in various ways one could give
a fair imitation of a train journey. Naturally, I visualised
the progress from station to station and was surprised by
the vividness of some of my recollected jaunts. I not only
saw the various scenes through which I had travelled but I
could hear them and smell them and sense their sunniness
or their humidity. How many of our experiences we forget
because the revivifying impulse is never encountered: yet if
the proper stimulus comes our way we can recall even the
least important of our dreams. . . . The fact that it is very
difficult to recall what a friend from youth looked like in
youth tends to suggest that mental images are 'localized'
and that a later image of a person 'displaces', or 'overlaps',
an earlier one.

FRIDAY 7

One of the necessities of art which many an artist takes
long to accept—or may never accept—is to wait for the
proper hour. Nothing should be forced or artificially stimulated—for the proper hour brings its own potency. Not that
the will is negativated thereby—for it is the will that must
build about the idea and with the power which the idea
brings. Not only may it be long before an artist accepts this
necessity of waiting—but it may be long, or not at all, before
an artist accept his final silence. Shakespeare's greatness is
augmented by his last years of accepted silence—so is the
greatness of Milton and Beethoven by their years of silence:
our own Shaw has not learned this lesson—nor the majority
of our novelists—nor poets like Masefield and Noyes.

SATURDAY 8

There is no question of the fact that we can sense the significance of a symbol without understanding what the significance may be. I had proof of this very decisively the other day. When looking at Hacker's 'Annunciation' I was especially attracted by the water-pot, and said as much in my letter to Lizette. Afterwards from Jung[2] I learned how much symbolism has gathered about the 'vas'. I learned from Jung also why I chose the whale as a symbol in 'Stanzas on Time'[3] and in the bairn-rhyme 'The Whale'.[4] Such illuminating explanation of one's own intuitive choosing is startling.

SUNDAY 9

Martin Smith called. Martin—in high metaphysical vein—which somewhat surprised me: yet why should one be surprised at the sudden manifestation of an unsuspected trait in a person—is not each of us close packed with seemingly unharmonious thoughts? Truly man is a microcosmos for within him is the earth epitomised—in every handful of dust is a potential world. Martin left at 4.0—having dropped from metaphysics to mercantile mechanics before leaving. Outside his little shop he intends to set up a 20-compartment 6*d*.-in-the-slot machine—the first in Perth. As pleased as a schoolboy—and we all joined in to help him ring the changes on the sixpennyworths one might get out of his robot Woolworth's.

FRIDAY 14

A Type. He is lanky, big-boned and with no colour. His voice bass; and when he greets you his smallish eyes seem to thrust themselves forward as if to share the handshake. His laugh is generous but without graduation and tends to finish in a draw-back which sounds like a resonant croak. He talks as if he were selling something to a buyer who is rather deaf. His conversation is hearty and topical and ever veers round to his own job. When he indulges in a philosophic aside it is common, axiomatic property or some contemporary phrase which has its season before another comes along. He is a natural and likeable fellow—but when he has said good-bye he has left nothing but the echo of a noise, and one forgets all about him until he returns again.

TUESDAY 18

A year ago when a young divine praised Pascal because (as he asserted) he had found certainty—I laughed to myself. Now I am realising that one must have faith in something definite (not mere faith in life) if one is to be able to gather up one's thought into some sort of whole. There must be the crystallising point.

MAY

TUESDAY 2

When one can no longer give free play to one's limbs the actions of others are followed with a more than normal intensity—so that one may enjoy movement vicariously, so to speak. Being a man it is the movements of women which have gained in attractiveness—so that to watch either Bella or Gladys hanging out clothes becomes an entertainment not without its so-called sex-appeal. It is but natural that an unnatural mode of life tends to proliferate through all one's being—and there is the grave danger of becoming sensually unbalanced. I know this danger only too well for I am blessed—or cursed—with a full-blooded virility which is incompatible with my stagnant bodily state.

THURSDAY 4

I know all your little faults of face and form but as I see you standing out there smiling—you are most beautiful. It is the fact of being 'out there' which makes you part of nature and of the imagination—so that both by adding and by taking away these create a different creature—and it is in like fashion that the lover looks on his mistress seeing in a single woman, and for some time, what those not in love may glimpse only in a propitious moment.

FRIDAY 5

These girls, with whom I still have contact, touch but the body of my being. That is an easy matter: but I wait for somebody who will set my mind on fire as well as my body: for my need is not to be loved but to love. Yet even here one must be careful not to seek for a vicarious salvation. . . . The acuteness of a cat's hearing. A cat was passing along the top of the McQueens' garden when I said Pizz!—I was astonished when it turned and stared about. Again and again I made the hissing noise and each time the cat stopped and looked. Distance 35 yds. or so and all windows shut.

SATURDAY 6
Jeffrey[5] and Montgomerie along about 3.30. . . . J. a very friendly fellow. A bad stutter when in the least animated: with his slightly protuberant eyes and mild manner one can picture him as having been a rather bullied schoolboy. Looked soft and loosely shapen beside the military upright and wiry-built M. I had to smile quietly to myself when they both got emphatic over the sterilization of the unfit—the paradoxical thing is that I look twice as healthy as either of them and yet I've crossed a line between health and disease over which there is no returning. Damned queer when one feels so healthy on what is—in the fulness of time—a deathbed. And what are you teaching me, M. and J.?—to attempt more.

TUESDAY 30
Too often, I am afraid, one might gather from these pages that I play the spider to my friends.

'Will you walk into my bedroom,' said the spider to the flies;
'Will you open out your spirits that I may anatomise
'With my little inky scalpel till each fad, or foible, lies
'Naked to the daylight or your own awaken'd eyes;
'Now I ask you,' says the spider, 'what are your replies?'
'Pick your own bones, Mr. Spider, won't you get a damn surprise,
'And when you've had your pickings you can leave them for the flies.'

WEDNESDAY 31
When one is more or less stagnant then one is liable to be tempted by fear: and thus, though I do not brood, I cannot escape all together these small devils who slide up and whisper the possibility of defeat. And the latest of these imps has suggested that my creative flow must slowly ebb since I no longer take the sunshine into my blood, and no

longer look on the moon or even a star: and, continues the sly fiend, here memory cannot help you for it is the actual flow of life from the sun and the planets which comes in like a sea to waken the pool of your own blood. But I shove the tempter away saying: 'You have been taking Lawrence too seriously; and anyhow poor Lawrence was in vital need of the sun.'

JUNE

MONDAY 19

The first review of *Seeds in the Wind* came along to-day—*The Glasgow Evening News*—Power[6] may have done it. Overpraised—but some truth too in it: certainly a good send-off to the verse. We badly need more poets and critics however—for with one book a man can make a bit of a name for himself here. Grieve—even allowing for his egocentricity—has not been helped by isolation: a number of men nearer his own calibre would have made it easier for him to keep balanced in his self-judgment and would have probably toned up his work—forcing upon him a more rigorous technique: but there must always be plenty lava and brimstone at the creation of a world.

WEDNESDAY 28

Perhaps the classic restraint which is natural to the form of my verse balances my romantic cast of thought—without the formal restraint I should have become liable to indulge in sentimentalism. As it is—in daily life I am continually experiencing the disappointment of the romantic. Not only in the common disillusionment of womanly beauty or childish innocence—but in the ordinary reciprocities of friendship. The romantic always expects too much. Yet there is genuine chagrin when even a normal expectancy is unfulfilled. A man, who has 'eaten our bread' for many years, yet has not bought one of my books—even for friendship's sake: a woman who would 'possess' me and yet her Xmas present is a cheap handkerchief which unstains in the wash—and so on. Verily 'most friendship is feigning'.

JULY

MONDAY 3

Read *Poems 1909–1925* by T. S. Eliot. I have never had any inclination to read Eliot's book but a whim prompted me to name it when Moll asked what book I'd like. I am afraid reading Eliot hasn't changed my preconceived idea of him. His poetry is rooted in a pedantic intellectuality: a waste-land verily: a valley of dry bones without any blood: there is wit—but the wit is also dry; brittle—no Rabelaisian sap: no human richness: only the false disillusionment of the young could model itself on this verse. . . . Whence these periods of lust? Have we whisper'd to the heart 'Now I am beyond love,' and this is the heart's retaliation? Indifferently we have looked on this woman and now we would say: 'Here is no pretence of spirituality—I would give you my lust.' Has this insistence no right of mutual expression?

TUESDAY 4

The heat and a blue-flies' hum recalled to me very vividly these moments—now composite—in which I lay on a banking of tall grasses when the heat made one ready for sleep: and not the heat alone but the dampish smell of earth and grass, and the bees' and the blue-flies' hum and perhaps the steady chirsh! chirsh! of the grasshoppers. Lying there so near to earth and to sleep, one partly laid aside one's individuality and became a warm piece of flesh and blood sensing the summer day directly and allowing the direct sensations free play upon the mind which now so naked to the elements seemed to be passive in a grave whose difference was only in being, and in feeling, earth watered with blood.

WEDNESDAY 5

We seek, often by rigorous suppression to curb the waywardness of passion—but it is life itself that can move or quieten us by a gesture. This woman, lovely enough, whom I may have desired vehemently and who by appearing suddenly at a distance has quickened the heart until its loud knocking would threaten its own walls—this woman—seen again, for a moment, in the half-light looking mildly from eyes which seemed sadly benignant and with a face so softened in the shadow—rebuked all former lust by her momentary beauty, so that the self made its self-confession, 'What evil prompted me to inhuman thought?'

SUNDAY 9

Martin Smith called. What sort of a human being am I? Here is a fellow-mortal who comes up in the hot afternoon to see me—and with painful feet: yet the feelings which I bear him are not particularly generous—nay, rather despairing: has he so few friends that he finds my company welcome; in what way do our spirits sometimes touch and harmonise. If we could pray would our cry not be, 'Make me more human; still more human.'

SATURDAY 15

Got Jim's imagination set agoing by suggesting that we ought to steal the Stone of Destiny—merely as a gesture to fire the cold patriotism of the people.

MONDAY 24

Men seem to find it compulsory to make a god of something—though they may often deceive themselves into the belief that they believe in nothing. When a really living faith is lost men turn to a trust in charms—hence today a recrudescence of disguised magic. The majority of men fear nothing more than to be wholly responsible for themselves—and if they no longer have faith in a presiding deity they doom themselves by a faith in numbers or some such fetish. It is a poor enough exchange to have lost even the God of Calvin and found the number 13.

AUGUST

FRIDAY 25

A Type? The easeful divine: with a body fitted for the most exacting labour he lolls back in the chair having written some pages of a sermon in the forenoon: my cigarettes are ready, my time is my own—am I not a fit philistine upon whom to try out the reverberations of biblical periods: a good point, Mr S—, you bring that quotation in nicely—ah

yes, one must not forget the individual application, etc.,
etc.: another cigarette and we are fishing or golfing or
munching yesterday's newspaper: one last cigarette—well!
just the last—and a few stories—have a care sir, that one
bordered dangerously on the bawdy: ha! ha! ha! that was
a jolly one – Ha! Ha! Good afternoon.

MONDAY 28
Whyte[7] phoned to say he'd bring F. G. Scott[8] along. . . .
I enjoyed Scott immensely: his mentor-relationship with
Grieve very interesting: a psychological touchstone: granting Scott's imaginative insight—why does Grieve depend so
much upon his criticism: the reflex in Scott's case—as it
seems to me—is to patronise Grieve: however, perhaps the
relationship keeps Grieve more balanced: I don't think Scott
is a big man—his penchant for song-setting rather suggests
that—but he is a very interesting type. I liked his straight
rather sardonic blue eyes: he is keenly alive.

TUESDAY 29
The most fruitful result from the meeting and mingling
with men who accomplish things is not so much to be
influenced by them along certain lines of thought—or by
accepting technical hints, etc.—but to be spurred on by
their example to strive to accomplish something of worth
also. It is the natural spiritual contact without compulsion
or coercion—which like a breath of life itself reinvigorates
and subtly challenges. Truly a man must confess that it is
the decency of men which helps to keep him decent and
the proximity of the creators which urges him on to greater
creative effort.

SEPTEMBER

TUESDAY 19
A Type: one became so conscious of his fear of being bettered
in any way by his fellows that one gradually realised that to
become personal seemed to be a rivalry; and ultimately one
grew content to listen to the other's mediocre moments of
glory; preferring to remain silent or impersonally conversational—rather than appear to be a protagonist for the

little dung-heap of self-justification. And not only was this thin-blooded fear of being bested an incentive to bolster up this flat life of mediocrity with scraps of municipal or churchy power but it also put a gag upon his praise—lest he should appear even more wanting thereby.

TUESDAY 26

I have been tempted of late to give up keeping a record of my dreams, and also my vocable verses. On the face of it such merely playful occupations ought not to be over-indulged in. Yet I do not think that the matter—in my case—can be so easily dismissed. If I were differently placed the question would have been settled by life itself—I shouldn't have had time for such idiosyncrasies. But as I have the time and as no other will probably ever leave a literary curiosity such as my vocable verses, I feel justified in continuing. There is also the additional incentive not to desist—the vocable verses give me practice in rhyming and indirectly help in ideological synthesis and in epigrammatic compression.

OCTOBER

FRIDAY 20

Though poetry is always symbolic, for it is but a part of reality which seeks to show the universal, yet the poet must be ever on his guard against esotericism. Truly to-day the esotericism of verse is in the over-intellectualisation of the symbol plus self-exploitation—it is what one might call a starved esotericism; but there is also the over-rich and recondite use of symbol which is at the polar extreme and may be called esoteric fatty-degeneration. This is Spenser's fault and Blake's; and is rarely absent in allegory which tends always to abstraction of the symbols which is death.

TUESDAY 31

Is not a man's identification of himself with a symbol a subtle form of self-flattery and a disguised boasting. Why, for example, do I associate myself with the unicorn—is it not because I would make claim in some measure to the attributes of that fabulous beast: even including its negative attributes, its solitariness and its self-will. But I also identify the unicorn with Scotland—and here we touch the quick of self-esteem: do I not hereby insinuate that in some measure I may be remembered by the new Scotland which is coming to birth and whose emblem I would claim to be the unicorn. . . . Finished *Capital*—the cenotaph of its subject.

NOVEMBER

FRIDAY 3 *Three Years*.

SATURDAY 4
Lest any who may, at some future date, turn over these pages and be tempted to sentimentalise upon the laconic note at the top of the previous page, let me confess that as I lifted my pen after writing it I found myself whistling: but without comfort, or calling, then might bitterness abide.

THURSDAY 9
The nearest counterpart to the physical joy between a man and a woman is that joy awakened by the mating of masculine mind and mind. This is a very rare joy—more pure—perhaps a little less human, more refined than passion: yet it cannot wholly escape the self—for the finding of one's thought echoed by another is a ratification of the selfhood; a subtle form of praise. This is inevitable and natural and is part of all human joy, physical or mental. Such a moment I experienced last night when I read Murry's article in *New Britain* on 'Shakespeare and Socialism'—I felt as if in my sonnet, 'To Marx', I had put Murry's prose into verse. Both the article and the sonnet must have been written practically at the same time.

THURSDAY 23
It was interesting, when reading Marx, to find that the idea of conflict—that is in a 'dialectical' sense—had been what I was intuitively seeking to explain in certain of the poems in *Conflict*[9] and elsewhere: *vide* 'The Lea'.[10] There is much truth in Hegel's 'thesis' and 'antithesis'—which, in so far as my own undogmatic conception of phenomena has judged,

is the only satisfactory summation of dualism. Nor, do I believe, is this metaphysic unwarrantable when applied to creative art wherein the form and the ideation—the shape and thought—reach harmony by a mutual striving with and against each other.

FRIDAY 24

One rarely hears a radio talk or reads an article on Scottish literature nowadays without meeting the Calvinistic bogey. Why has our art been so meagre for 100s of years—*ergo* because of Calvinism: and that's that. But surely we are over-easily contented with this solution which is but half-a-solution. Must we not go on and admit that there is something very congenial to Calvinism in the Scottish psyche—even our land and climate have something in common with the stern creed of Geneva. One does not turn round and blame a cramping creed in itself but the men who submit to it. If for far too long Scotland has accepted Calvinism—there can be no doubt but that at one time, and for a lengthy period, Calvinism was acceptable.

DECEMBER

FRIDAY 8

It is not surprising to find the poetry of our age is lyrical—for the lyric is the natural vehicle of changeability of mood and our time must be one of the 'moodiest' in world history. Assured of nothing we snatch at the momentary glimpses of reality afforded us and seek to gather some sort of foundation for faith from the accumulation of the evanescent fragments of truth happened upon. This ever indeterminateness of our mood is sufficient for the lyric poet, but affords only an arbitrary conception of reality—so that his work can be 'selected' and have unity—but seems lacking in unity when 'collected'.

CHAPTER FIVE

— 1934 —

JANUARY

THURSDAY 11

It is the sympathetic imagination of man that approaches the godlike: only by this are we able, in a degree, to enter the life of another and partially live it. This is the attribute by which we sweep up with the bird against the wind, climb the cataract with the salmon, curl out upon the grass with the earth-worm. But above all it is the sympathetic imagination which enables us to experience, in some measure, along with our fellows and by so experiencing we are kept sane in the whole meaning of the word. It is this attribute which is most evident in genius of a high order—and marks the pre-eminence of Shakespeare and the drama: and it is its vicarious nature which makes the drama man's truly communal art.

TUESDAY 23

All of us have, even if we are able to keep it a secret, a high opinion of ourselves which is a natural if facile complement to the fact that each of us is unique. Yet alongside of this self-satisfaction is another secret which is more rarely confided—the assumption that few of our fellows can be as foolish as we are in our solitary phantasies: which of us has not suddenly paused in the midst of his whimsies and thought: 'Is it possible that another mortal has indulged in so impossible imaginings ranging through all the passions with protean delight or irritability: is it at all likely that I am made to play the puppet in the day-dreams of my friends even as here they posture in my own?'

42

FEBRUARY

THURSDAY 15

In reverie, as in dream, we not only indulge in a fanciful
ego-satisfaction but sometimes deceive the self from realising
the true significance of the imaginary act. Thus, once or
twice, I have found myself, in day-dream, stricken by
some deadly trouble to which I must succumb within a
year or so. I persuade my doctor to hide the truth from the
folks—and to advise a complete change. Whereupon, with
a faithful nurse (preferably youngish and of comely looks,
of course) I hie me to some lonely northern isle. There I
spend my remaining months of life—preparing my MSS.
for publication, etc. And what does all this melodramatic
stoicism amount to—merely a most brave solution of a life
problem by leaving it.

MARCH

THURSDAY 8

I suppose it is a cliché; yet it was only to-day (9th) that
I spontaneously thought, or experienced if you like, the
phrase: 'Snow is the garment of silence.' The garden upon
which we look may be in quiet, yet with the falling of the
snow we become aware of the silence as if it were a presence:
the scurry of the flakes by suggesting sound makes the
stillness not an absence of noise but a 'manifestation' of
silence—snow makes stillness a positive experience. And
this unfulfilment of expectancy is always the shifting away
of emphasis from negative experiences—thus, in part, death
and time became possessed of positivity in the mind of
man.

SUNDAY 18

We have, in all probability, an indirect proof of the reciprocity of genius and people in the fact that the great
man is always of his time—he is both for the age and
for all ages. And this should lead us to a more balanced
judgment—so that we are not tempted to expect more of
genius than the individual—in his hour—can give. The

potency of the individual contribution must be assessed not only in its achievement but in its potential influence on the following generation. I think when we realise this we shall put a truer value on the work of Lawrence, for example. His achievement was to be the passional antithesis to intellectualism, and his potent legacy is in manifesting to us the necessity of creating a balance between the intellect and the blood.

APRIL

THURSDAY 5

The dissension from orthodoxy of so many honest and enquiring minds to-day is not a wilful action but a natural growth: the danger for some is somewhat akin to that of the outcast devil who wandered thr' the waste places and found no rest—and whose return to his first home is an aggravation of the originally evil state. Has Eliot, for example, not returned from the 'Waste Land' back to a more dogmatic climate—his latest book, *After Strange Gods*, is almost priggish in tone; and slightly medieval. I do not suggest that his attitude is valueless—it is, I fancy, a necessary corrective: he is as it were the bridle on the Laurentian stallion, and if we assess his significance thus we are in no danger of retreating. The danger for others is to ignore orthodoxy altogether and dissipate their energies in an anarchic flux of action.

SUNDAY 8

It is significant that the most important English poet in the first quarter of our century should have written so much in prose: I mean Lawrence, of course. No doubt there was an impatient element in his make-up which was loath to submit itself to the discipline of verse—but that is not the important factor. It was the age, in which Lawrence reached maturity, which failed him and made him too a partial failure. The war was, and to a degree still is, the symbol of our cultural disintegration and religious unfaith. Lawrence had neither the cultural background nor the religious assurance necessary for a great poet. We are yet

in a toppling world and much has to happen before great
art will be possible again.

FRIDAY 27
A diary is like drink; we tend to indulge in it over often:
it becomes a habit which would ever seduce us to say more
than we ought to say and more than we have the experiential
qualifications to state. It is a kind of private paper which
demands its quota of news every day and not rarely becomes
a mere recorder of spiritual journalese. But not only can it
persuade us to betray the self—it tempts us to betray our
fellows also, becoming thereby an *alter ego* sharing with us
the denigrations which we would be ashamed of voicing
aloud: a diary is an assassin's cloak which we wear when
we stab a comrade in the back with a pen. And here is this
diary proving its culpability even to its own harm—for how
much on this page is true to the others?

MAY

THURSDAY 3
A type: Short and 'tubby' with a fresh unlined face for his
odd 30 years, and something of the artist about his longish
nose. Relieves himself of a thought with startling suddenness
and with as startling a suddenness switches from one thought
to another. Worries about his soul and yet, the fact that it is
not his very soul that worries suggests that he will become
ever more and more soulful as his body becomes more and
more solid. His religion is the supremacy of the spirit by
the denial of reality to matter, and this assumption leads
him into his most melodramatic annunciations. Thus with a
lifted forefinger he will warn us that if, at this very moment,
he had a sufficiently powerful soul-consciousness he would
vanish from our sight. But we are not impressed as we look
on his ruddy corpulence.

WEDNESDAY 9
The mind of man is a queer museum in the corners of which
we come upon unexpected oddities; ever the individual
happens upon quaint grotesques when moving through his

own mind in reverie—here is a gargoyle which grinned at me from a dull coign yesterday:

> Right modest is Matilda Smart
> Who blushes at her lonely fart.

It is natural, it would seem, for man to find a rich source of humour in the body's necessary functions and this is partially due to the fact that a man is so often at the mercy of his body: the body takes the proud spirit down a peg. But I also believe that much humour is concentrated in natural excretory functioning to divert the intellect from sexual functioning and the exercising of the wit in obscenity.

JUNE

THURSDAY 14

Copies of *The Solitary Way*[1] came along: looks quite nice. Looking at this handful of lyrics of unequal quality one is tempted to question if they are worth all the bother of publication. Yet a glimpse of life may be reflected here and there which might have been unrecorded by any other intelligence. One's own mind becomes strange even to oneself—taking in the colour of the day, while the careful self is unaware, until the stain of the contemporary spirit is in the very blood upon which the self survives. Then by a gesture the self is at last startled into the recognition of the change which has been evolving about it—and accepts the folly of seeking to halt. Thus I have lost my solicitude for poetry, knowing that there are times when life must assert itself over art.

SATURDAY 30

Just as car was leaving at 3.0, Jeffrey came in. . . . A very nice fellow. Senses the frustration in the air too—but not strongly: his delight in the classics still potent and seemingly an inspiration yet. Moving among men, and with his domestic responsibilities, it is but natural that he feels socially fulfilled to a large measure outside of his poetry—whereas if I grow in power as a poet my social functioning must be through verse: and yet if one is made unquestionably aware of the futility of art at this hour—what then?

JULY

WEDNESDAY 4

One dangerous concomitant of ratiocination is the tendency to work away from the nucleus of reality which is ours—out to sweeping circumferences that embrace sufferings and endurances beyond our selfhood; and not only so, but from this speculative philosophising we take comfort and even self-content: we fight for man in fancy and applaud our good intentions. I am afraid that many brave words have been set down in these diaries which are—for myself—no more than words. If I have learned something of necessity, something of acceptance, even a modicum of endurance—what do I know of a necessity which proclaims itself daily in the roar of wheels, in the fall of the pick, or the noise of idle feet: have I not entered a cell made too comfortable by the service of my fellows?

AUGUST

WEDNESDAY 15

It is the necessity of social life which has helped to make and to keep men human. If it had been possible for mankind to survive as isolated individuals we should, in all probability, be still in the jungle. It has become fashionable to sneer at the herd-instinct and to commend the independence of the individual—but, if the herd has its faults, we cannot deny that if it is to function at all creatively it demands qualities more elevated than such as solitariness requires. Without the submergence of the self in co-operative action many of the altruistic virtues could not have become a part of human nature—for tho' the family has done much to humanise man, it required the larger fellowship to make him truly human.

SUNDAY 26

If you ask me why I deem it worth while to fill up a page such as this day by day—shall I not reply, 'Worth-whileness hasn't very much to do with it'? The most natural reply might be, 'Because I cannot go out and chop a basket of firewood or take the weeds out of the garden-path.' Yet that wouldn't be a wholly honest answer. We are all sustained at times by the thought that whatever we may be we are certainly a solitary manifestation of creation; not a single other creature in all the history of the world has been just as our self—not another will be like us. Why not put on record something of the world as seen by this lonely 'ego': here and there perhaps a sentence may be born whose father is reality.

SEPTEMBER

SUNDAY 9

One is rooted in the world by having one's roots firmly in one's native earth. A creative mind is very often stimulated by strange scenes and peoples—and certain minds need such stimulation—but the greatest find their strength in their own land. There would seem to be a real reciprocity between a man and the earth from which he has grown, so that in its fields and cities he has all the material that his mind requires; and that only against this 'local' background can he see the light of eternity clearly—broken into the variable colours of earth and thought. This is noticeable even in verse translation where the translator tends to transpose the foreign setting into the semblance of locality.

WEDNESDAY 12

In art one does not really know what one is going to do. The ground plan is there but the structure evolves with the building—so that the finest sections of a poem, for example, are felicitous findings during the construction. It is only when the work is under way that the necessary adjustments, elaborations or curtailments, can present themselves to the creating intelligence which controls and yet submits to the structural and psychic necessity. Perhaps from this the Scottish poet may learn how to approach the solution of his linguistic problems (if at all soluble). He will not sit down to 'work out' ways and means—but will work them out as he tackles his subject-matter in Scots.

FRIDAY 21

There can be a too ready acceptance—even of necessity; and sometimes I feel that if I had loved the outside world more fervently I should have known a more fervent regret for its loss. Being at ease, one may accept the ease with the necessity; so that the desire for sharing in the life of day becomes weak; even the desire to enjoy the sun and the hill, the sea and the wind and the stars, dies down; the comfortable cell—the safe hermitage—the easy peace—these tend to seduce the spirit; the very acceptance of necessity which to an outsider looks like courage may prove to be weakness—a weakness which confesses to the self, 'This is now the life which I would not lose': thereby confessing to a shrunken spirit which prefers a garden to a world.

SATURDAY 22

If we assume that there is a God then we cannot pre-suppose that he exists in isolation—all things must be related and inter-related with Him. Nor can we accept—if we believe in the 'being' of God at all—a wholly impersonal pantheism. All things manifest God and are sustained by him—and in some sense (possibly as a work is related to its maker), He is in all things; yet the mind is not content to halt there; over and above all is the selfhood of deity, capable of complete solitariness—yet incapable of a purposive existence without His creation.

OCTOBER

MONDAY 8

Assuming that in the beginning was God—perfect and alone; then so isolated in his perfection how could he know growth, and without change how could he learn what manner of being he was? Assuming this, we are led on to reason that out of the desire for self-knowledge God set about the externalisation of his self—which we call creation. But in sub-human nature he had but exteriorised his perfect self, for all was bound by the laws which he had imposed, and had personality in no real sense. If then

God was to challenge himself, it was necessary to create a creature which was not only subject to 'determinism' but had a will of its own. And thus man was made 'in the image of God' and by man's sin and folly God learned to be loving, long-suffering, and pitiful: without man, there could be no God of love.

THURSDAY II

Whatever significance Jesus may have for us we must indeed recognise that his saviourhood has, at least, a symbolic significance. Many, no doubt, assume that the spirit of man has made him a wish-fulfilment—but whatever interpretation we may put upon him we cannot get away from the fact that the majority of men not only desire to be saved from the self—but seek out salvation by various ways. A few see their 'escape' in art, some hope to be saved by a woman, some believe that in nature they will find peace—all quests are emblematic of the need for salvation tho' sometimes one may not be fully conscious of the why and wherefore. The need is fundamentally religious, and to-day the way of salvation for many is the communal state. This also, of course, will be but a phase—the quest can never end.

MONDAY I5

There is a reason for the excesses of creative minds of which the average man may be wholly unaware. The reason is no excuse, of course, but I presume only the most balanced intelligences have at no time succumbed to the mood. It is a kind of exhilarative reaction after the completion of a task; almost a form of disintegration after concentration—a mental relaxation which tends to loosen moral control, for with the relaxation is also the residue of mental excitability left over from the task. The mood is a very complicated one compounded of feelings of joy, abandon, power and goodwill. In such a moment the artist is urged to indulge the body—the most natural reaction to mental excitement—thus he gets drunk or turns to women.

THURSDAY I8

Much of Georgian poetry was an escape—a kind of truancy into the country—which proved its lack of reality by the large percentage of merely descriptive verse. This flight from industrialism and its problems could be but a phase; and today when the urgency for a solution to our economic and social maladjustments walks the streets like a judgment, a turning away to a rural lyricism is no longer a pardonable truancy but a cowardly retreat. It is in the challenging light of the social crisis that we must examine the contemporary revival of vernacular verse in Scotland. It has behind it a genuine impulse—a desire to test the possibilities of the canon—but it brings with it the dangerous seduction of taking refuge in the womb of the past and calling it a rebirth.

NOVEMBER

TUESDAY 13
Against the limited horizon of a room little things tend to become disproportionate—such things as food, cigarettes, etc.: but the greatest tendency is in the disproportioning of the self. One is so adjusted to a minimal environment and all in the environment has been so adjusted to the self—so that one might claim that every shadow falls just as one desires and every book and chair keeps its appointed place: and every day almost is made a robot—that the tendency is to become centred in a cell rather than in a world. And a concomitant is that one is apt to judge persons overmuch in detail—seeing them in 'close-ups' rather than against the background of the outside world. In short the danger of the comfortable prisoner is to expect the world to conform to the regulations of his cell.

SUNDAY 18
No department of the mind's activity can have a quarrel with another so long as it seeks to name reality within the radius of its power. It is when one section would impose itself on another, and would claim authority outside its capabilities, that clashes arise. Thus we find an antagonism between science and religion—when science would interfere beyond fact and when religion would deny fact. There is likewise an incipient rivalry between philosophy and poetry when each

forgets the true nature of its functioning. The philosopher in so far as is humanly possible must build up his system step by step ever stressing the rational nature of man: the poet does not argue but sets up a sign of the oneness of the moment and of eternity: there is a philosophy in poetry and a poetry in philosophy—but each is an attitude of the mind and not a method.

SUNDAY 25

Our ideal state can be, of course, only that state in which the individual is given the best opportunities of fulfilling his self-hood; even an ideal state cannot live one's life for one. If then we see that we can approach nearer to the realisation of the best kind of state by achieving a classless society, let us be assured that we are not fighting merely for a class but for all—the rich are perhaps thwarted as much by their wealth from realising their self-hood as the poor by their poverty. It is not therefore out of vindictiveness that the new state must grow, but out of a fundamental brotherliness which strives not for a class but for humanity. The poor know their plight—the rich are in greater danger—made complacent by comfort.

DECEMBER

WEDNESDAY 26

Even after we have gathered together all the facts that might appear to mitigate our usefulness to the world—and it is childishly easy to collect excuses—we are, if we are honest, forced to agree that one is in need of no single specific incentive to produce something; even if it were only a song. No doubt it is a help to have friendly encouragement, to have lively experiences, to see lovely countries and great cities—in short the creative impulse tends to be stimulated by all these things. But the essential urge is not a dependent upon vicissitude; this spark of life within a man lives or dies with the spirit which is wedded to it—it is the self-hood that turns either lifeward or deathward: the life is there and it is we who must learn to use it.

CHAPTER SIX

— 1935 —

JANUARY

FRIDAY 4

Now that I am growing older and can see young folks
isolated from me by a number of years I am sometimes
halted by the thought, when looking on them: 'Is it a fact
that my own youth ended at 24?' This, of course, is a time
when the joys of physical freedom are emphasised and the
pleasures that gather around a home of one's own. And with
the emphasis comes the thought that we are but human once
and that to be able to joy in action is a great privilege. The
thought of course is but fleeting—for it is folly to brood:
and has not one known the joy—which is enough; and are
there not many who have never known it?

SATURDAY 5

I suppose that it was man's recognition that he had to
submit so often to necessity which started his thoughts
towards the problem of free-will and doom. It is indeed
difficult to escape the conclusion that our life is urged on
by necessity and that without the twin needs of hunger
and love we should be creatures unrecognizable as humans.
And is it not in our willingness to become the bondsmen
of necessity that we grow in humanity—so long as we do
not confuse necessity and selfish lust. It is indeed in our
response to necessity that we are made aware of our oneness
with the race and that our need is something greater than a
personal desire. And here we again approach the mystery
of the finding of the self by losing it.

MONDAY 7

Whatever one's circumstance—therein one can see the
reflection of the social state for the symbols of life are
also in dead things. Thus from my own estate I look
beyond the range of the eye; and I am moulded by what
I may not see. Here I can learn that comfort has its chains
of silk which are linked to the chains of poverty: here I may
learn the wisdom of necessity which teaches men when to
act and when action is folly; and here most of all, perhaps,
I learn the interdependence of us all—so that at last a man
is forced to confess that he is sustained by the charity of
life; and with this realisation comes, especially at this time
of social chaos, the challenge: 'What is a handful of words
to the hungry mouths of men?'

WEDNESDAY 9

Let us content ourselves knowing that we may be doing the
will of heaven, and are worthy of a blessing, even when
called to be but an old ladies' companion—attentive to
Mrs G.'s report of her sister-in-law's bladder-trouble—or
of Mrs S.'s shopping crusade—or rather her argonautica,
from which she brought back in triumph the bridge-coatee
not too large to be called an outsize.

MONDAY 14

A character: He was a stocky little man who jerked his
words out with a jerk of his body. Standing there, with
his leggings on and his belly stuck out; and flinging
away his words with a swinging uplift of the head, he
seemed to be a powerful bird with clothes on, and this
impression was furthered when his head came into profile
showing the bold sweep of the prominent nose, and the
smallish brow above surmounted by its tuft of hair. His
conversational hobby was the infelicities of matrimony—an
epithalamic fugue in which the wail and the warning
answered one another. It was a half-serious, half-playful
recrimination—for the performer had been hastened into
a childless marriage by the fear of premature paternity, yet
still retained a tenderness for these months of prenuptial
passion.

SUNDAY 27

Snow makes us aware of silence for in such a multitudinous
falling we expect sound. Snow also illustrates the paradox
of the fascination of 'varying monotony': this steady falling
of similars which yet are so wayward in their fall. In like
manner we can watch the oncome of the tide, the flow of
traffic in a busy street or listen to the sound of a stream.
And sound suggests that a measure of the attractiveness of
poetry is in the variation of a monotony; so that the ear
is kept expectant—knowing the tempo and intrigued by
the modifications. The 'monotone' in music—especially in
dance music—is of course a fixed ground bass—so to speak:
and much of our delight in jazz is just this consciousness of
the monotony behind the melody.

FEBRUARY

SUNDAY 10

I wonder if it is insensitivity, or a sense of proportion, which
has left me little enough disturbed by the death of Gibbon.[1]
The news was shocking—for Gibbon was comparatively
young—but it did not touch those impersonal centres
which respond to a national loss. And yet, in a degree,
Gibbon's death is a national loss—why then was I not
more deeply touched? Perhaps the reason is two-fold: I
myself am still too apathetic towards Nationalism—and as
a writer Gibbon meant practically nothing to me. We seem
all so small literary persons and there are so many human
beings for whom no man has yet spoken. It would seem to
be an hour of waiting—the travail has begun—but the time
of birth is not yet: and can the writer be born before the
quickening of the communal spirit?

MONDAY 11

Reading over the adjoining note, on Gibbon's death, to-day
leaves me with a feeling of inhumanity. If I could have
sensed it with a more sympathetic imagination I should
not have written a note like that: there was a gusto about
the man which no other contemporary Scottish novelist

possesses. What is the cause of our hardness of heart? Have we, in the words of Lawrence, not the 'courage of our tenderness': are we too afraid of giving our self away? One might also add, personally, that to be over-dependent is to become a receiver rather than a giver: and we are made human only by sharing. Thus one upon whom responsibility is at a minimum is always in danger of becoming unhuman—the intimacy of human contact is often shunned not because of self-sufficiency but because of the fear of responsibility.

MONDAY 18

A Type: Her virginity has a barren quality like a tree which will never blossom; her body is a bare tree—straight, bony, without sap—there is no suggestion of the potentialities of spring: even her hair hangs like strips of bark. Tho' undesirable one is yet sometimes—for her own sake—tempted to lay a hand on her; sensing, perhaps in truth, that she hoards the wish to be manhandled—almost brutally. She might awaken then. But there she sits drumming out a wooden sound upon the chair, and her own voice going on and on as if mechanically; even, unemotional—a record turning in her head almost alienated from her being. And when she yawns—which is often—she seems to be yawning at herself; desire in her appearing to be so minimal that her yawn cannot suggest even the desire for air.

TUESDAY 19

As I was washing myself this morning—my belly to be exact—I suddenly thought why not make the rhythm of the machine basic for a poem on the machine. A ship's engine, the wheels of a train, etc., seem to fall into a rhythm of four beats with the ictus on the second beat, and a much slighter stress on the last beat—   I have noticed that this is the rhythm which one hears also at our local water-works in Tay St. No doubt there is quite a simple mechanical explanation of it—but to me it is the rhythm of the machine. If this rhythm proves at all suitable for a poem on the machine, I fancy that the basic line will be one of 12 syllables; and the difficulty will be in avoiding the ordinary Alexandrine effect.

MARCH

SATURDAY 2

Advance copy of *Brief Words*² came along; looks very
well—scarcely anything that could be improved upon—excepting the actual contents. I can understand something of
a woman's feelings on seeing her child. There is a sense of
accomplishment (even if what has been done is ordinary
enough), the satisfaction of knowing that a process has been
completed; a desire at last made tangible; a memorial of a
phase which, if yet doomed by change, is more durable
than memory. Thus, like a woman, I would lift up this
little creation and look and handle it—a thing cut off from
the self and yet part of it: an ambassador however frail sent
out into the world from the secrecy of solitude.

TUESDAY 5

If I had not been blessed, in youth, with an athletic
fleetness, if I had not known the joy of leaping and dancing,
if I had not known these moments of exhilaration when one's
only expression of the knowledge that it is good to be alive is
to strain the body to exhaustion—then I might have been
tempted now to despise the pride of mere physical fitness,
to sneer at the daily adulation of the boxer, or the football
player, or the tennis star. But having known the same pride
in youth—the sheer muscular exuberance which forces one
to run against the wind or to lay hold of a friend and bear
him to the ground—having known this I am saved from
jealousy and cannot betray the body by denying that it is
a fine thing to feel the life that is in flesh. Even yet I can
feel it—as if a statue grown warm, not bitter, with the desire
to run.

APRIL

SUNDAY 7

Finished *Sunset Song*.³ No doubt at all about the richness,
the routhiness of this book. Careless, often unnecessarily
'coarse' to employ his own far too much over-worked word,
but the humanity is there and the bright objectiveness which
is the need of modern art.

FRIDAY 19

It was indeed most wise of the Church to baptise so much of paganism, as it were, into the service of Christianity: to transmogrify the naturalism of the ancients into holy acts: to incorporate much of the worship of the old gods into the recognition of the new. Indeed if the Church had foolishly revolted against the nature worship of paganism, the barrenness of transcendentalism would have made Christianity the creed of a sect and ultimately—cut off by its very nature from common people—it must have died. But its marriage with the best in pagan worship kept it rooted deep in earth and, who knows, it was this fit unity which kept the figure of Jesus human—never losing the man in the God.

WEDNESDAY 24

Perhaps the strangest sensation which the self can experience is the strangeness of the self. This is rarely a wholly wakeful feeling but is sensed either on waking from sleep or from day-dream. Not a few times now I have known it, as if some part of one—which was yet not implicated in the self—stood aloof from both the body and the self and by such a detachment became a judge. At least in my own experience I am not conscious of 'this man' wholly dispassionately. I tend to see him as not only a stranger but one not entirely pardonable for his strangeness. It comes in part, no doubt, from the returning consciousness which, made aware of this body stretched upon the bed, grows also aware that even when fully awake it will continue to lie like a body asleep.

MAY

SUNDAY 5

Fundamentally, I suppose, we ought to ask for no other justification for living than the fact that we are here with our fellows upon an earth which daily demands our response. But the very distance of the stars must have stirred the earliest men to speculation. The indifferent regularity of the heavens and the proximity of flux: the steady assurance symbolised in the heavens and the deathful instability of human life. Out of these, perhaps, came the desire for permanency—the desire to be for ever a part of life; hence the evolution of a God in whom we all might abide: and which of us even yet would not be a memory in the eternal mind? Thus we must be for ever imposing reason upon reality—and perhaps we would be less than human if we were not so driven by desire.

MONDAY 20

The natural response to intellectual tension is to indulge in some form of physical exuberance; the nadir of which is to drink or eat overmuch. I recall that one evening in my first year at Edinburgh, after having written a poem which I thought was very good at the time—but which I destroyed later—I was so charged with physical exuberance that I dashed out of the house and walked swiftly through the streets in a downpour of rain. In a sense it is a manifestation of joy and without it the cycle of creation is not wholly completed. Not that the lack of it is of much importance—but there is perhaps a tendency to grow stale when the physical participation is wholly wanting. Joy is, of course, a mental state—but like all human moods it is not isolated from the flesh and without a bodily complement—is rather like a kiss on paper.

JUNE

MONDAY 3

A blackbird whistling in the rain: he must be the Caruso of the tribe—I could have listened to him for hours the interplay of notes was so varied, defiant, witty, confident, merry, bold—anything but melancholy. Just when it was almost too late I thought I'd note down his wurlywas—but found it well-nigh impossible to catch the sound and transpose into syllables at the moment: one would have to listen for a long time—but here is the rough and ready transcription: chickee-chickee-chee: ti-ti-ti-titty-titty: chittie-cheea: tweeto-tweeto-tweeto: what-ya-doin', what-ya-doin': hullo-hullo-hullo: chejoey-chejoey-what-what-what: gee-up, gee-up, hoo-hoo-hoo: get away, get away, get away; you would,

you would, you would, would you?: hoi-hoi-hoi—have-a-
look-at-me. . . . Well—you are worth looking at, too.

TUESDAY 4

TO MY DIARY
(on a dull day)

> Since verse has power to give a grace
> Even to the commonplace
> I shall, within a rhyme, declare
> The cupboard of my mind is bare
> Not only of an underdone
> Cutlet of thought; the very bone
> Of prosy platitude is gone.
> And since for you, my hungry hound,
> No meaty morsel can be found;
> And since I would not have you own
> A master who could proffer none,
> I bleed myself to be your drink:
> Is not the blood of poets—ink?

WEDNESDAY 5
Merely as a natural fact (though out of it comes the
spiritual? moral? or whatever adjective one prefers) we
recognise that we do not belong to ourself. The life within
us is only coloured by our selfhood: when we act spontaneously we have passed beyond the choosing of the self.
There are moments in every life when the life within us
seems so to decide. Thus it spoke in me, after I had learned
the nature of my trouble, when suddenly I halted in the
dusk beside the pillars of West St George's, Edinburgh,
and stood for a moment bareheaded saying over to myself
'Now I can be a poet.' It is life's recognition of itself and a
salute to the necessity centred at the core of life: and out of
this recognition is born a rock of acceptance on which the
selfhood can retain its peace within all the changeableness
that daily darkens with doubts and vain imaginings.

WEDNESDAY 19
Sometimes one is perturbed, when looking back over a
stretch of years, to find how little has been won from
experience. Thus I look at my two years in the Navy and
my four years at the University and wonder what meaning

they have given to my days. Often one is tempted to imagine that these were well-nigh lost years contributing little—but the fault must be in the experiencing self. It is so difficult to lay a hand on the dead years—the dust of the trivial and the momentous are so mingled: how is one to sort them out? Was it necessary to serve two years with the fleet to learn that men are often by no means 'calm and collected' by 30; and to sit in the shadow of a University for four years to learn that there the love of learning is of far less importance than the preparation for teaching?

MONDAY 24

Art can be propagandist only to a limited degree and if constrained (as it has been in Russia) to a definite cult, must in time become sterile. It is an aspect of the temporal and the eternal—a symbolic problem. Everything may be symbolic—but not all can retain their symbolic content: there is a local and contemporaneous element about man's activities and symbols which are rooted only in human deed must necessarily become impotent. At the moment the action being a necessity—a life demand—is vital; but it is transient and being non-recurrent (like flowers, tides, etc.), becomes, by fulfilment, its own tombstone. Thus propagandist literature is essentially of the same estate as that private symbolism of the poets who substitute their inner life for the world. It is a strange perversity to come upon this monopolisation of art in the comrades of communism.

JULY

WEDNESDAY 3

I suppose one ought to be flattered when the attitude of a friend would confess that he thinks more of one's self than of one's work: and yet isn't the selfhood more solicitous for the work than for the self? Be that as it may—I have found more than once that individuals who have introduced themselves, on the strength of the delight which some of my verses appear to have given them, very rarely betray a marked enthusiasm for my verses after they have settled down as

accepted friends. Not that I encourage the discussion of
my verses in the least—for I have no very high opinion of
most of them—but one cannot escape the conclusion that,
even if these individuals are honest enough, and I believe
that they are, what they really needed wasn't more poetry
but more companionship: and in the end it is easier to give
a man a poem than a satisfactory mutuality: perhaps my
social responsibility is partially fulfilled in ways I but dimly
apprehend.

MONDAY 8

Sometimes I am surprised when I realise that I am at least
a potential poet—for I do not appear to feel experience
strongly enough. Perhaps many protest over much: be that
as it may I could not possibly, with any honesty, confess to
the intensity of feeling which many declare. Every other
day someone or other asserts his or her passion for music,
scenery, country, literature or perhaps a game—and I am
forced to turn to myself and say: 'And by what are you so
deeply stirred?': and I am afraid I should have to confess
that it is only the rare moment that arrests me. Perhaps my
seeming, or real, indifference may be summed up by saying
that I am lacking in loving kindness: yet perhaps also we are
often stirred more deeply than we realise, and to be stirred
over-easily tends to preclude the possibility of ever being
stirred so very profoundly.

TUESDAY 18

On the green where the bread is broadcast the larger birds
come down—and first the crows and the seagulls eat up
the larger pieces—then follow the starlings and last of all
the sparrows picking up the tiniest crumbs; and looking
on this gradation of satisfaction are we not too satisfied by
the natural justice—to each according to his capacity? Is it
not also thus with experience—so that he who is able to
accept most experiences most? And if our life is a legacy
of mediocre memories, we must not blame life who casts his
experiential bread broadcast for all to share. And does it not
fall richly enough, even on a back-green, if the mind which
looks forth is hungry enough for life: but if we are sparrows
let us not cry out upon life for not being greater birds.

TUESDAY 30

Confessio Jonae. Truly I must be the very Jonas of invalid-ism—threatening the ship of pity (not that anyone would welcome it). But I must surprise the stranger who comes with compassion—lying here like a rubicund warrior taking his rest. In general health I seem so much superior to many of my visitors and within my radius of action so much more muscular. I get passing pats from genial souls for my uncomplainingness—but what have I to shout about now that I am so physically at ease? One feels merely like a strong man who is subtly bound with chains that do not chafe. Yet there is the psychological aspect and it is there where danger is. One dreams too much, trifles too much, thinks of women too much, is too easily irritated by small things, is too little disturbed by the world outside, is too ready to excuse the self: and what of this confession—is it not made too easily, too glibly, too contentedly?

WEDNESDAY 31

Merry thought:—'The busy, bonded, blundering, bar-bottomed bee.' 'The bagpipe's blethery, bucolic, bubbly-joking bourdonary.' 'James Joyce's joky-poky jesuistic-dolorosa juju.' Perhaps this alphabetical word-play is a *reductio ad absurdum* of Joyce's method illustrating—or rather suggesting—the possible amalgam of the ludicrous and the true and, for the mind rich in language, as Joyce, a method of fostering the most bizarre associations. But the method is obviously an insuperable seduction from the truth since it lends itself primarily as a medium for wit and its progeny, sarcasm, exaggeration, fantasticism and blasphemy. What Joyce seems to confess by his style is that he would make the flesh a word and his sensations thoughts. His world is now inside his head and his true audience only himself.

AUGUST

TUESDAY 20

A persona. . . . He belongs to the flamboyants; life and humanness are in him: he forces us to confess: 'I would not change this man—for his waving flame has its own intriguing twist.' His speech comes from him in a low and rather monotonous rumble—flowing as it were over his lower lip which is large and pendulous and thrust forward as if by the steady stream of words. From time to time he gets up to come nearer or to emphasise what he is saying and as he speaks he tends to keep his head down and slightly to the side—not with the appearance of self-consciousness or from any unwillingness to look one in the face, but rather as if he were listening carefully to the murmur of his over-flowing syllables.

WEDNESDAY 28
The cry of the writer to-day ought to be: 'How can I achieve simplicity?' Perhaps at no other time in history has it been more difficult to be simple. The world is now at every door—and, even if we admit that the needs of the human spirit are a constant, the complexity of modern sensation tempts the writer to be complex; and to assume that 'difficult' writing is axiomatic with profundity. But may we not learn from nature, what she herself would seem to have been forced to learn, that simplicity of structure is the secret of survival (and by simplicity is not meant bareness—but directness, clean-cutness, harmoniousness; the smooth action of a bone in its socket, which is not without much subtle adaptation). Let us but seek to make thought and impression fit thus—so that a poem may be as communicative as a gesture.

SATURDAY 31
What we generally get from a book is knowledge and only at rare intervals experience and I presume the difference is the old one of reason and emotion. In the former we are persuaded by logic, accepting a truth which we have not 'proved upon our pulses' but which satisfies the intellect; in the latter we are moved as by a scene of natural beauty, a face, an animal gesture: something within us seems to meet the utterance and fuse into a moment of reality which we recognise and would proclaim. It is thus that my 'Variations on themes' originate—certain phrases become

an experience such as, in ordinary circumstances, I might meet in the streets, in the open, or in my intercommunion with men and women. The truth must be there even on the printed page or I could not be stirred into experience.

SEPTEMBER

TUESDAY 3

STABS IN MY OWN BACK

Soutar the poet used to lie
And watch the butterflies pass by;
And with a mild, abstracted air
Unto himself he would declare:
'These are eternal thoughts: I watch 'em
But damn'd if I can ever catch 'em.'

Soutar the poet used to lie
And brood upon divinity;
Until, in meditative birth,
This aphorism was bodied forth:—
'God and humanity are one.'
He took his pen to write it down;
But, having heard the front-door bell,
Shut fast his book and mutter'd: 'Hell!'

OCTOBER

SATURDAY 5

IMPROMPTU CONFESSION

Soutar the poet often said
To the sole-self beyond the self:
'Are we, who share this quiet bed,
Upon the turret or the shelf?

'Sometimes I deem this living hearse
Is as a hot-bed to assure
Our few and fragile seeds of verse
May be unfolded into flower.'

> But the sole-self who loves to tease
> Replied with metaphysic wit:
> 'I pawned our body to dis-ease
> And bought ease with the deficit.'

SUNDAY 20

MORE STABS IN MY OWN BACK:—EPITAPHS

> Bill Soutar, the poet of Perth,
> Here shifted his bed under earth:
> He was married to Art,
> A most troublesome tart,
> Whose brats were not very much worth.

ANOTHER OF THE SAME:—

> For thirty years Bill Soutar pined
> Upon his death-bed lying:
> The children which he left behind
> Were not so long adying.

ANOTHER OF THE SAME:—

> Wull Soutar wi' the muse was thrang
> And monie bairns she bore him:
> But he lay dwinin' for sae lang
> That they were deid afore him.

SATURDAY 26

I was awakened at 3.0 a.m. (this morning, 27th) with an instantaneous suddenness—by the falling of a piece of burned-out coal which struck the fire-guard forcibly. This peremptory awakening set me thinking; and I came to the conclusion that we are summoned back into consciousness by such stimuli as do not immediately explain themselves to the subconscious for what they actually are, or diguisedly in a dream. We might say, figuratively, that we waken ourselves by coming up against an associational dead-wall. A loud-striking clock, to which we are accustomed, does not normally waken us or call forth a dream—the subconscious recognises it for what it is. Bodily postures if not too uncomfortable are 'explained away' by dreams; it is therefore legitimate enough to claim that certain dreams are the guardians of sleep. We may also assume that animals are kept on the alert during sleep by reason of their associative paucity.

NOVEMBER

TUESDAY 5

There is an acceptance of mediocrity which is an honest facing of the truth. We learn from experience that we can accomplish certain things but that there are many things which we are not talented enough to attempt. Such a relinquishment is often a humiliating gesture for the self—while yet we are young enough and retain what, in the final analysis, is but selfish ambition. In truth, we may assert that half of the regret inherent in the acceptance of our own limitations comes from the realisation that our acceptance is the valediction to our youth. But there is also an acceptance of mediocrity which is mean-spirited. Then we are comforted by the thought that we abide secure behind the shell of our nonentity. Since we face no risks we have the greater comfort: since we are content not to aspire—we cannot fall.

WEDNESDAY 6

Aloofness may be traced back to the desire to abide in the womb—there is peace because one is shut in wholly from the sensory world. This is the nadir of being and no more than a warm consciousness of oblivion. From this analogy we learn that it is only by multifarious contact that the mind can attain to a comprehensive knowledge of itself—for action must ever be the final arbiter of the intelligence.

SATURDAY 9

What I gather from the few poems of Hopkins that I have read is that the passion in his verse is predominantly intellectual and has a tortured quality about it indicative almost of an unnatural construction of the body: and this may be so as Hopkins was a Jesuit priest. There is the temptation, of course, to read back from personal fact—but his very persistence in abiding so constricted testifies to the predominance of the intellect in his make-up. Not that his poetry is a twisted thing—but the balance which it has achieved is as a precariously-perched climber arrived at a peak by a most exhausting effort—sheer will forcing on the eager but not over-robust body. The antithesis of a Hopkins is a Byron; and it is symptomatic of the intellectual phase thr' which we have been passing that the poetry of Hopkins has been so stimulating an influence.

WEDNESDAY 20

'When we cannot hear what the day is saying we turn and speak to the self.' True, but something of the daylight may be in us also. Our own life would make us wise if we were but willing to stand away from our self for a moment and look upon our history in detachment. What may such a glimpse teach myself? Surely that the spirit of man is stronger than his chains. From a world I entered a university, from a quadrangle I came into a garden, from a garden into a house, from a room into a bed—only a coffin can complete the 'cellular series'.[4] Yet—granting the paucity of achievement—my mind has continued to grow and if growth is not maintained the thwarting element will be in myself. I should have no doubt functioned differently if the world had remained there from which to choose—but the potential (core of our self) cannot be smothered by environment.

DECEMBER

SUNDAY 15

One is sometimes tempted to ask why there are no epic poets to-day: but the answer is fairly obvious. The epic must be built upon a sure architectonic and to-day there would seem to be nothing which can offer such a structure. All our beliefs are in flux and consequently our philosophy is a fractional thing: we are baulked of the cosmic sense which must pervade the epic. Unless we can polarise our thoughts between earth and 'heaven' we can but build

towers of Babel—and this is manifested in the work of Joyce
for example. Thus even our one epic theme to-day—the
history of man (interpreted, say, in the light of the Marxian
economic) being but a time-theme, is a truncated thing; and
until, in some way, we are able to polarise it with eternity we
cannot hope to achieve an epical expression.

SATURDAY 21
Surely it is not so rare an experience in the life of the
majority of us—to be suddenly aware of a desire to bless
either a scene, or a flock of birds, or a company of
people. The origin of such an emotion must be in the
comprehensiveness of our looking—the beauty and the
truth of reality is in the moment, tho' it is impossible for
the individual mind to say why it is so; one can but testify
to the illumination—to the realisation that at this moment
we looked with visionary eyes. Such being so we are forced
to accept that all life is ever before the eyes of God in such
a moment of eternity—beyond good and evil.

CHAPTER SEVEN

— 1936 —

JANUARY

SUNDAY 12

I realise now that I would marry if I could do so; but I am not wholly blind to the fact that my arrival at this nuptial mood has been accelerated by adventitious means. What woman —granting she overlook my disabilities—could expect that my affection was entirely unselfish. Yet—and this is perhaps a confession of my overweening self-regard rather than of my confidence in the magnanimity of women—I do believe that a woman would accept me for what I am and that our marriage should be one of mutual affection and not a 'second-best' accommodation for security and comfort. No doubt to an outsider it must appear preposterous that at my age I should consider it not an impossibility to win the affection of such a woman as I might have reasonably hoped to have won when a whole man; but the hope is there and places me, I suppose, among the incorrigible.

SUNDAY 19

Had Aldous Huxley been as richly endowed with imagination as with intellectual penetration his *Brave New World* might have been a truly creative challenge to our machine age. But, lacking the moral indignation and the humanising solicitude of Swift, he fails in his Savage to create a real sponsor for humanity. And the superficiality of his philosophy is shown by the final scene. The Savage, in the office of Mond, had demanded for men the full inheritance of earth—the right not only to happiness but to misery; the right to share in all the experiences natural to a man.

And even the orgy in which he was an actor ought to have been, in spite of self-despisal and remorse, but another, if negative, exhortation for the need of maintaining his human qualities. His suicide was a blasphemous denial of all that he had represented.

TUESDAY 21

If one could but gather in all the significances of that solitary bare branch against the sky—the mind would find itself centred in reality. So are all things burdened with truth if we have but the ready mind, and the only meaning which eternity can hold for a human intelligence is a state in which such moments of intuition as we now and again experience here are continuous; where every grass-blade is a manifestation of universal harmony and every flower the quintessence of a cosmos. Thus all things can teach us wisdom and nothing natural is without profundity; and all the common intercourse between men, which appears so often mean and trivial, is yet rich with significance to a mind that has learned not to impose itself upon experience.

FEBRUARY

FRIDAY 28

When we accept Keats' interpretation of what he calls 'negative capability' we must be on our guard against assuming that it is a kind of insouciance. The negativeness is really a response—it is the readiness of the being to accept life with no dogmatic assumptions; and from this passive receptiveness to learn how to act creatively. It is a willingness to be guided by the event and not to set up any ideal by which we would judge beforehand: it is, in short, submission to experience. This is a relationship between the individual and vicissitude: but as a citizen it is difficult to see how one can retain such an attitude towards social change. For good or ill we must act in anticipation there. Thus, today, we cannot rest in a state of doubt about War, Socialism, or the Machine: we must act in anticipation for or against.

MARCH

TUESDAY 10

What diarist has not, at some moment, become ashamed of the numerous entries which belittle a friend or slight an acquaintance?; and yet at the time the man or the woman appeared so and had by words and gestures irritated the writer. And the nature of the entry is also a self-confession to the diarist's own moods and limitations; so that even if he return to these pages, which now accuse him, and efface their nay-saying, would the action not testify rather to a fear than to a generous impulse: would not the solicitude be primarily for the diarist's own good name? I shall leave all my entries even such as may shame me—for I do not hate anyone; and I know that the moments of human sympathy are not rare. Mutual irritation, boredom and actual antagonism are unavoidable; but at heart we all desire to like people and to be liked.

THURSDAY 12

To have the consciousness of death ever as a distant background to the day may be so far from morbidness that it has a creative, or at least harmonising quality: we are forever being reminded that our life is transitory and uncertain, and that we journey through the world but once. And this admonitory certainty has the power of constraining us from inhuman action; under the necessity of daily death we become more sensitive to the need for human tenderness. When our earthy sojourn is relatively so short what greater folly than to aggravate the miseries of man by our modicum of inhumanity.

SUNDAY 22

Only at certain moments is the crow a sinister-looking bird; and how much of its ominousness is not a mere human imposition. I like the bluff, proletarian, chested walk—like a boxer, or footballer with his hands in his pockets. Then, who would not admire his determined but unhurried approach to a tit-bit; and the assured attack after the claw has been set so firmly. Here too he reminds us of a workman who knows his job and goes about it confidently. But—lest we admire him rather than like him—he is not always bold and self-assured. Timidity sometimes overtakes him and he sidles up to a piece of bread as if it were a bomb: then how laughable the sudden peck and the backward leap.

MONDAY 30

When one considers how comparatively short are our days upon earth; and how comparatively uneventful and unmeaningful our individuality—one is surprised that we are content to keep our relationship with one another so circumscribed and trite. We gather together and talk of generalities: we turn over and over merely the conversational rag-bag. We know almost all that is to be exchanged and our communion is wholly uncreative; we are but rarely experiencing even at second-hand. It is true that there is always some modicum of sympathetic human interchange—but all is kept within a little compass of mutual comfort and regard. One wonders if it were not wise to begin to front—or affront—one another with disturbing queries: to break down the little social walls and see one another against the background of eternity where all queries are legitimate.

APRIL

SATURDAY 4

How we are apt to forget the multifarious life which is gathered within a little plot of ground. The ever-changing intensity of light and colour, the restless play of brightness and shade upon the hedge, the steady arrival and departure of bird and insect. On such a fresh spring day as this it were easy to stare from dawn to evening and allow the living flux to draw our thought from us like a slow emptying of consciousness until we were but men of sense: motionless pillars of sensitivity within a calm sea of colour and sound. Are we not baptised thus into a like calm and washed, unwittingly, from the accumulated crust of self-consciousness: made one for the hour with the day; and strengthened as by a sunny sleep? For the comforting of the mind is won by the communion of earth with earth; our dust having its own need and its thoughtless wisdom.

TUESDAY 14

No matter how excellent one's reason for engaging in a war—the result is ever a denial of the integrity of the individual; it is a deliberate choosing of force in preference to faith in life. War is the negation of trust and, for all its bravery, the child of fear: it seeks to win salvation by offering the body as a proxy for the soul. By its very nature it must drive men into its service—for it can no longer claim their faith: and where there is no faith there must be coercion. Faith is individual and seeks for no proof—and how can it be given to a man or forced upon him? Men are conscripted for death, but reality must be experienced by the solitary selfhood. . . .

WEDNESDAY 15

A pacifist cannot compromise but must accept that the use of arms is wrong under all conditions; and that any deliberate manifestation of force is wrong. He may, as an individual, break his own ruling when faced with some private challenge to act—such an occasion were an exception, to prove his humanity: there is always, individually, the exceptional situation in which to act merely from principle were unhuman: organised retaliation is the antithesis. But if the pacifist must accept no compromise: neither should the combatants expect compromise. The history of warfare tends more and more to show that it is folly to expect a limitation in the use of destructive material. By what fine discrimination are we to agree that a certain kind of poison gas is a legitimate weapon and another is not? Yet this desire to set a limit—however muddled as logic—is evidence of man's humanity and a gesture of brotherhood even from the claw of destruction.

TUESDAY 21

FOR ANY FRIEND:—
(IMPROMPTU CONFESSION)

Friend, if your ghost should ever peer
Upon your portrait sketched-in here,
Be not dismayed, nor fret, nor rage,

If you should find a certain page
Retains, what you would fain untrace,
Only the foibles of your face.
Turn to another leaf; and there
Discover that you also were
Like to the being which you sought,
And found, within your private thought.
Were it not insult (man or woman)
To paint you less, or more, than human:
Were it not scornful to the earth
To embrave you better than your birth
Or baser than your hope? Then peer
And learn, O ghost, I too am here;
For with your image I put down
An illumination of my own.

MAY

SUNDAY 3

There is a dual function in writing: one deliberate and the other epiphenomenal; one self-controlled and the other indeterminable; one willed and the other gratuitous: in other words a man in writing what he wants to say is at the same time exploring that region of his mind which is beyond selfhood—and, as he writes, he sometimes comes upon fortuitous phrases which are discoveries outwith reasoning. But, albeit these illuminative findings are in a sense gratuitous, they are also the rewards of exploration: it is when a writer has set his mind in a certain direction and is 'about his business' that suddenly the happy discovery, revelation—call it what you will—is come by: we must indeed—to adopt Anatole France's phrase—go forth lamp in hand if we are to meet and recognise reality.

FRIDAY 8

In so far as a man is a true poet, so far is poetry an experience: it cannot be taught. One may recognise that certain 'tricks of the trade' are demoded and others are coming into being—but to adapt oneself merely by a rational recognition must inevitably lead to falsity and if persisted in may wholly undermine the writer's self-confidence. The poet must both grow into his poetry and grow out of it—and if he is guided at all it can be no more than a predilectionary influence; facing him, as it were, towards the necessity for change—but the actual change must grow out of personal experience. Thus the true poet though willing to submit to criticism is not deeply influenced by it; and aware of the fundamentally 'private' nature of change is neither greatly elated by praise nor depressed by censure.

SUNDAY 24

If at 20 I ever considered what sort of man I should be in another 20 years—I am certain I visualised a much different person from the one who now writes. In many ways I am so little changed from the youth of 20. It is true I know myself much better but I should hesitate to say that it is a much better self that I know. Still the childish mood may possess one, still the romantic day-dream divert, still the fretfulness and the peevishness of youth can, at moments, master one, and more powerful than at any other time can a passionate thought make the body of a woman the most desirable thing in all the world. Yet this at least I have outgrown—to look upon poetry as a consolation: there is no consolation—only acceptance of life and of the limitations of the self.

JUNE

TUESDAY 2

The odds and ends of an evening's conversation which remain in the memory next day may seem to be the merest trivialities—and in themselves so many of them are. A disastrous hair-cut, a kirkly squabble, an indisposition and the like: but we are insensitive observers of a scene if we are aware of only the superficialities. Behind the personal and the trite one can sense the values which give even the asides of a commonplace conversation a live human significance. The triviality is so often rooted deep in human worth. And thus behind our three examples one may glimpse an œsthetic sensibility, a moral standard, and a brave heart. Wisdom is not an isolated thing but a growth sustained by these very commonplace communications of everyday.

FRIDAY 5

I had a most decisive proof to-day that I am colour-blind to
certain shades. Mother remarked on the fine blooms which
were on a couple of azaleas which the gardener put in this
season. I hadn't noticed them. They are a flamy pink shade
and seem little different to me from the light green foliage:
indeed the rich green of the calceolaria plants beyond are
lovelier to me. At a distance even dark red doesn't impose
itself on me forcibly.

SATURDAY 13

Sometimes one is halted by the thought of mortality when
looking upon a woman who, tho' she may not have awakened
our love in youth, yet attracted us: and now we are halted
perhaps by some fleeting expression and recall that this was
the face which we had kissed and the body we had touched.
A few years have gone and we no longer desire to touch and
we may be surprised that we ever so desired. Yet stranger
still is that memory which reminds us of those other women
who died while yet they were young—even without our
love they yet took something of our being into the dust:
the memory of them is almost impersonal—we are sorry
that youth may die. But is not the bitterness of a lover
forgetful of the impersonality of love also—he is perhaps
old and disconsolate but there are innumerable lovers who
are young and who relive the memories which he can but
regret.

WEDNESDAY 24

Finished reading *Grey Granite*[1] by Grassic Gibbon. Hasn't
the richness of *Sunset Song* but has much of its verve. One
is ever conscious of a certain rank liveliness about G.'s work:
much of it fermentive—like manure: indeed we might claim
that most of his writing was a rich manure which would have
fed the growing seed of his thought had he but lived. He was
getting rid of much in these books; and it is a great pity he
did not live to fulfil himself. He was the most potentially
Scottish novelist since the war.

MONDAY 29

A lame cadger who stayed near C—was fond of a dram
and often came home singing-fou'—his horse needing no

guidance. On these occasions the cadger invariably lay in
the bottom of his cart bawling out a stave of his own
composing—a genealogical jingle, so to speak. Here it
is:—

> My faither's deid; my mither's dottle;
> Jimmy's* daft and I'm cripple.[2]

SEPTEMBER

TUESDAY 8

There is a 'worthy' minister at Redgarton, the Rev Dauvit
Grahame who is rather too fond of his dram; and some
years ago he was called up before his session. When the
meeting was about to begin Grahame jumped up and said:
'Gentlemen, a preliminary word, please. I am well aware
why you have summoned me here this evening but allow
me to ask two questions before we proceed. First, has any
man among you assisted me home when I have been the
worse of liquor? And second, is there any man among you
whom I have *not* assisted home when he was the worse of
liquor?' As the answer to both questions proved to be in
the negative, the Rev Dauvit turned about—and no doubt
left for the inn at Pitcairngreen.

FRIDAY 11

BETWEEN TWO WORLDS

> Wha wad pu' the rose o' the south
> Gin oor white rose were in fleur;
> Or hae an auld sang in his mouth
> Gin oor words cud mak a newer?
>
> Tak hert for there is monie a rit,
> Sae deep in the broken yird,
> As draw it a' thegither yet
> And mak a hame for the bird.

* brother.

> But we can never hale oor hurt,
> Nor sing a sang o' oor ain:
> Or we lay by oor geary sturt
> And bide as brither men.

SUNDAY 13

Sometimes one recognises oneself as a representative creature, a symptom, a symbol—even if but the veriest gesture of a period. I live in an age which is truly between two worlds and this has been intensified about my own private world both by nationality (sic) and circumstance. As a Scottish writer (ditto) I am set between the two associative worlds of the English and Scots tongues: as a mere appendage to class I occupy a kind of social limbo between the proletariat and the lower middle class: and as a crock I am chained between inactivity and the memory of action. Such a status is a peculiar challenge to the imagination; and I am afraid I have as yet barely begun to accept that challenge. The acceptance will be, in so far as I am even but a veriest gesture of a period, a vicarious answer.

WEDNESDAY 23

The pre-eminent writer must have three qualities in his work and these are pity, tenderness, terror. The pity which comes from magnanimity, the tenderness which comes from courage and the terror which comes from the recognition of life's grandeur. It is difficult to define this use of the word terror for the fear is not in the recognition but in the possibility of failing to respond creatively to the magnificence of life. Shakespeare, of course, has all three qualities, as has Milton though Milton is deficient in pity: Burns has no terror (in the above interpretation) in his poetry and Dunbar has little tenderness; perhaps only in the isolated *Testament of Cresseid* of Henryson do we find the three necessities of great poetry gathered together into one Scottish poem of magnitude.

OCTOBER

SUNDAY 25

Who, looking abroad upon the world to-day, were able to retain his faith in humanity if his trust were centred merely upon the humanity of man? If our trust is in the will of man alone then our god becomes the State—and, alas, we now have more than ample evidence of the inhumanity which comes from such adoration. Power is the prime attribute when the state is idealised and the ultimate criterion of value is force: it is the apotheosis of possessions over individual worth. But the antithesis of this materialism is not individualism but individuality—which is the recognition that the individual is a manifestation of value and co-operates directly with life (in theological language, with God). Our least dogmatic declaration of faith is therefore that we act for life when our acts are uncoercive and that every such act—however infinitesimal—has a value which is incorporated into life and survives the individual.

FRIDAY 30

A Scottish poet writing in English is aware that there is a foreign nuance in his use of the southern tongue; an elusive quality which cannot be isolated and is yet sensed. And this quality, it would seem, so colours all his verse in English that the critic of the south is unconsciously biassed towards such poems as have assimilated most perfectly the English tone. It would appear that he is subconsciously insensitive to the Scottishness—or confused by it. Yet he can confront a poem in Scots with keen discrimination even where he is at an associational disadvantage. Perhaps the difference in approach is—allowing for differences in poetic quality—due mainly in the latter instance to the lack of preconceived notions and traditional standards.

NOVEMBER

MONDAY 2

Would not many of our Marxists liberate us from one dogma merely to chain us all the more securely to another? Dialectic, though it is measurement, is not the measure of life nor is it an explanation. Man himself is a determinant—and this human factor is what is so often ignored by the Marxist. And it is due to this ignoration that the dogmatic Marxist can forget the individual in the class and thereby fail to differentiate between hating a system productive of classes and hating our fellow-beings. It is a strange faith which can advocate the necessity for hate in a crusade for brotherhood. But the Marxist has become so enamoured of his thesis and antithesis that he would force life into *his* system; and the consequence of all such arbitrariness is always an inhuman and inhumane act.

SATURDAY 7

A handless joiner in a little country shop near Dunkeld was making a proper botch of a window when his master came over to see how he was getting on. 'My God, man!' he exclaimed, 'could you show me a worse windy nor that?' 'Aye,' answered the botcher, 'there's ane ablow my binch.'[3]

DECEMBER

WEDNESDAY 16

Sometimes out of frustration, out of our own inadequacy, out of our self-pity, out of our childish pride, out of our unwillingness to submit to reality—sometimes from this multiple pettiness our blood is darkened by hate at the end of the day. Then the accumulation of insignificant thwartings seems to gather in the heart blocking the free flow of the blood. Then the mind darkens and is made lurid by destructive thoughts: we become a spectator of the disintegration of our sanity looking upon a secret drama in which all our passions posture in our own shape. Time halts while we stare in horrified fascination until some demoniac gesture so repels us that we remember our humanity and dismiss the degenerate drama with the light of reason. Slowly the hardened heart is mollified; slowly the chaos of the mind is ordered; slowly the beneficence of sleep drowses us into oblivion.

SATURDAY 26

This was the first occasion on which Jennie the new maid gave me my tea. As she went out I said: 'Leave the door a little open, Jennie.' Whereupon she piped back cheerily, 'Righto, Willie.' So, yet again, it would seem I retain a semblance of youth sufficient enough to elicit a spontaneous christian-naming even from 17. Yet the grey is in the hair and the Shakespearean frontal already immanent and the light and shade of maturity gathering on the face—if youth remains it is on the mouth: tra-la! even yet the edges curl up.

CHAPTER EIGHT

— 1937 —

JANUARY

SUNDAY 3

Our gravest sin against life may not be in our deeds but in our lack of response—in common language our hardness of heart. This is the chronic condition of self-regard for our callousness may not be a deliberate desire to hurt or to ignore others; yet in order that our own life may escape implication, in order that we may not suffer or be distressed, we set a restraint upon our spontaneity until at last restraint becomes our response. Such are those who in Lawrence's words have not 'the courage of their tenderness'. But it is better that the heart should bleed than that it should become a stone able to confront life only by hardening itself into indifference.

THURSDAY 7

There are moments which might be called 'moments of magnanimous lust' when one is made conscious of the many ageing virgins who have never known the touch of a man upon them; and with the thought comes the desire to awaken them so that they return to the dust with at least one memory of passionate intimacy. This no doubt is the very nadir of a romantic mood—and not without a modicum of male self-deception; yet even in the sharing of the body alone there can be true tenderness so that no hate remains in the remembrance of the moment. This is the leaven of wholesomeness in the carnality of Burns: the women whom he knew were remembered with tenderness and what might have been hate was transmuted into song.

This is not the justification of lust, for life demands more than a song.

MARCH

THURSDAY 11

I am well aware, of course, that my insistence upon the 'money complex' in a capitalistic society is prompted, in part, by my own 'indebtedness' to money. Had I been in a less comfortable environment, even the little creative work which I have done might not have been done—and, most certainly, would still be practically all in manuscript. But the admission in no way invalidates the fact that value has been seduced by money-value; even if my reaction to the complex were itself a complex, it would still be a condemnation. The recognition, however, is necessary for one's own personal integrity—for it enables one to adopt a more unbiassed attitude to one's art. While one has to admit that even the very small recognition which one has achieved has been in large measure 'bought', then one is fairly adequately protected against an overweening opinion of one's efforts.

SUNDAY 14

THE DREAM: (A BYRONIC BALLAD)

There was a Scottish publisher
(So loud the breeze doth blow)
Who gave a poet bread and beer
And the bright money O!

He took a trumpet in his hand
(So loud the breeze doth blow)
And sent a blast through fair Scotland,
Tra-la and tirraloo!

And when he woke the people's ears
(So loud the breeze doth blow)
This prince of all the publishers
Brought forth a folio.

He chanted from his mighty mouth
(So loud the breeze doth blow)
To east and west, to north and south,
To lordly folk and low.

It was the poet's words he spake
(So loud the breeze doth blow):
Sleep on, poor poet, do not wake,
Your trumpeter sleepeth too.

FRIDAY 19

How plainly we can recall the things which we handled
as a boy. I was about 7 years old when I got my first
fishing-rod, a yellow-painted wand of cheap wood—price
sixpence—but it had the look of the real thing. Proudly
I marched on to the upper harbour and prepared to drop
a worm into the 'bloody-hole'. This historic feeding place
for eels was so named as into it flowed all the refuse from
the slaughter-house across the street. I had just baited my
hook when a much older boy, Robertson, with more or
less forcible persuasion, commandeered the rod under the
pretext that he wanted to show me exactly how to catch
an eel. Certainly it wasn't long before he had hooked a
large one—but his sudden jerk up was too much for my
yellow impostor which promptly snapped in two and left
me lamenting.

SATURDAY 20

And this is what I daily take for granted:—Teeth-water
at 6.45. Shaving gear thereafter. Fire lit: breakfast and
newspaper: subscription to nature's 'pirlie-pig' collected:
washing-water: feet dusted and bed made: my table, and
all its accessories, lifted over: room dusted: fire kept
going: dinner: 'water-works': fire kept going—odd job
now and then. Tea: 'water-works': wireless put on for
news: fire kept going: spot of supper: wireless: table etc.
lifted back: teeth-water and accessories: 'water-works':
foot-pads shifted and bed clothes arranged: fire still burning
brightly—and so to bed about 11 or 11.30. This the mere
'necessities'—but there are the many extras: personal extras
such as leg-washing, hair-cutting, etc.: and the general
extras such as entertaining friends, getting messages: and

the cleaning of linen. A well-nigh endless list—and this is
what I daily take for granted.

APRIL

THURSDAY 8

Mr Keith and a cigar came in. How naturally the 'money
nexus' can be accepted. Mr Keith, speaking of some Aber-
deen friends (please note, there was not a trace of bitterness
in his voice): 'We had a very pleasant reunion—not having
come into contact with them for many years. You see, they
did very well during the war and left our circle; but they lost
a lot of their money and came back to our level again.'

SATURDAY 17

About 3.30 C. M. G.[1] came striding in resplendent in full
Highland rig-out. He had been celebrating his descent
upon the South—but hadn't reached the blethering stage
so we had a hearty time, with much loud laughter. He
had a number of MSS. with him and read part of his
Red Scotland,[2] which sounded quite convincing. As he
read he supported himself at an angle over my table and
the angle increased with the reading until he was literally
dropping cigarette-ash and dialectical materialism all about
me. I thought it might relieve the congestion if he removed
his plaid—but discovered that it was part of the regalia.

WEDNESDAY 28

GENETHLIAC CHANT

This is the day whan I was born:
Tak pity on my mither:
I hae the saul o' a unicorn:
Tak pity on my faither.

I micht hae learn'd a handy trade:
Tak pity on the lairish:
But I'm a penniless poet instead:
Tak pity on the parish.

I micht hae bade a briny boy:
Tak pity on my hurdies:

I micht hae been somebody's joy:
Tak pity on the birdies.

The wind blaws north and the wind blaws south
Wi' naither brank nor brechin:
The Lord has pit a sang in my mouth
That micht hae been a sechin.

MAY

SATURDAY 8

Are we not reminded yet again, by this bright uprush of
flower and leaf, this green and coloured foaming which yet is
poised and holds its shape—are we not reminded that every
moment is a moment in eternity. The isolation, however
necessary for the comprehending sense, is an arbitrary
circumscription—the individual thing is but a cell in the
body of life. Yet though there is an arbitrariness about
isolation—the mind is made wise by contemplating the
forms of things if it sees in them the symbols of reality;
there is the need for structure in the manifestations of
flux; and the most potent symbols of life embody both.
This also is the criterion of art—that its formality be as a
momentary poising of flux; a wave in curve, and not a mere
cup imprisoning the water of life.

SUNDAY 16

Russell McQueen (referring to *Junior Reader in Scots*): 'I
see Rabbie Burns is coming on now—he's included in the
same anthology as you.'

MONDAY 17

It is so easy for the creative mind, aware of the vicarious
nature of art, to assume that art has a peculiar value and
that the artist by remaining true to his craft may be granted
peculiar social privileges; may be indeed excused for all sorts
of eccentricities and anti-social indulgences. But the truth
is that a man's art cannot be isolated from his common
intercourse, and the more human his relationship with his
fellows the more generous his work. However imposing may
be the creations of genius—let us never forget that they are

founded upon the common experiences and intercourse of men; and that the individual gift can grow to fulness only when it is nourished by a magnanimity learned from communality.

WEDNESDAY 26

I suppose that every craftsman arrives at a moment when he asks the self: 'What good is it all? Is there not something unnatural about the life of an artist?' This mood is no doubt partly conditioned by the fact that art means so little to many; and the artist looked upon as a queer being who busies himself at a kind of game: all right, perhaps, to keep a fellow from wearying—but professionally an excuse, more or less, for not doing an honest job. And the attitude cannot be dismissed high-handedly, especially in a world where so many need bread and where art has grown so epiphytic. But the mood is also conditioned by what might be termed 'the Rimbaudian urge'—to be free of the need to recreate reality and to become a part of tangible existence: to share a common, appointed task; a wife and children to return to at the end of the day; and the simple, social intercourse of ordinary folk. Perhaps a Rimbaud could achieve such a reorientation and retain his integrity, but for the majority of craftsmen it would be the betrayal of their birthright.

JUNE

MONDAY 14

The only logical alternative to a God is the isolated individual; for if we deny that life is a unity and is purposive, we can set up no comparable integrity other than the unification of experience in the individual mind. But to accept this necessity is to accept only the reality of the self and its moment; and such a polarised cosmos can claim no validity beyond the isolated self. Rather would the imagination teach us that the integrity of the self is maintained by its polarisation with a reality which sustains the universe; and that only by the submission of the isolated life of the self to the experiential teaching of life can the self learn wisdom.

JULY

AUTOBIOGRAPHY[3]

Out of the darkness of the womb
Into a bed, into a room:
Out of a garden into a town,
And to a country, and up and down
The earth; the touch of women and men
And back into a garden again:
Into a garden; into a room;
Into a bed and into a tomb;
And the darkness of the world's womb.

TUESDAY 13

IMPROMPTU IN AN EREMITIC MOOD

I am William who would hearken
For the small and stilly voice;
But the breezy bodies come and go
In love with their own noise;
Yet I try to be a Christian
And salute the bugling words
Though I envy gardener Adam
When his brothers were the birds.

I share matrimonial sagas
And the tricks of all the trades;
The soliloquies of parsons;
The confessions of old-maids:
Yet I try to be a Christian
And indulge the rigmarole;
Though I envy Luke the lazar
Who was lifted from his hole.

Ah! forgive me, fellow-creatures,
If I mock when you are gone;
And if sometimes at life's concert
I would rather sit alone:
Yet I try to be a Christian
And applaud the tootling talk;
Though I envy paralytics
Who take up their beds and walk.

THURSDAY 15

Anecdottle: There was a foreman in Pullars called—if I remember rightly—Willie Low. When my mother was a child he was an elderly man who had outlived two wives but was courting one of the work-girls. Having made up his mind to propose he took his fancy for a walk up Jeanfield way and suggested that they might wander through the grounds of Wellshill cemetery. He ultimately led the girl to the grave which held his dead spouses and, as they stood looking down at the stone, he said: 'How would you like to lie there, Maggie?' and Maggie accepted this unique proposal by answering: 'Fine.' I believe that this story is already a legend—but the above is fact.[4]

AUGUST

SUNDAY I

One of the most sanifying 'exposures' for Scotland would be the tracing-back to its roots of our assumed meanness. I have little doubt that so-called 'Aberdonianness' is symptomatic of a general meanness of national spirit accumulative since our loss of nationhood. By the severance of our continental ties, our linguistic roots, our traditional heritage, it was inevitable that parochialism should spread like a national blight, so that ultimately our national traits have withered into idiosyncrasies and our types degenerated into 'characters'. A land famous in time past for heroes, scholars and martyrs is now symbolised by kilted comedians, long-faced elders and grasping yokels.

MONDAY 2

IMPROMPTU ON THE QUITE IMPOSSIBLE SHE

> This is the kind o' wife I wud wed
> Though I dout she'll no be in my bed:
> Better owre strappan nor owre sma':
> Better owre steerie nor owre slaw:
> Better owre youthie nor owre auld:
> Better owre couthie nor owre cauld:
> Better owre easy nor owre strack:
> Better owre snoddit nor owre slack:
> Better owre breistit nor owre spare:

Better owre swarthy nor owre fair:
Better owre gabless nor owre gash:
Better owre rogie nor owre lash:
Better owre hameart nor owre gaun:
Better owre tenty nor owre blaw'n:
Better owre merry nor owre mimp:
Better owre loavish nor owre skrimp:
Better owre dawtie nor owre dour:
Better owre sautie nor owre sour:
This is the kind o' wife I wud wed
Though I dout she'll no be in my bed.

WEDNESDAY 18

Always we return into our isolation as sound must return to silence. However numerous our contacts with men and women we are still aware of a gulf between us that nothing can bridge. Suddenly the moment of solitary comprehension returns and we see our self and this other as unique creatures each with his own centre of sensitivity which cannot be shared: this little tower of aloneness from which each looks upon the world. And though, by life's teaching, more and more of our common humanness can be shared with others yet, by necessity, our own private world becomes more and more isolated by the uniquity of experience. So that, at last, even if we may be able to say with conviction: 'I love all the world,' we hide behind our breast another world which none can see.

THURSDAY 19

Even if the mind had at last to give up its faith—not merely in a future life, conditioned by life here, but also in a beneficent mind sustaining the cosmos—even then purpose would not be removed from life upon earth nor value become only an arbitrary standard. If we should look upon nature and find an expressionless face, we should still learn from our human intercourse that certain actions are deathly and that others give life and more abundantly. Faith, too, would remain; but a faith so orientated that its hope would be in man's destiny, in that we should have to accept the responsibility of God realising that the blind urge of life was striving towards fullness through us. This is the only purposive alternative to a belief in God—and is, seen rationally, less 'balanced'.

SEPTEMBER

WEDNESDAY I
There are certain mythological creatures that have a probability of their own—they do not appear to us to be incongruous and magical; we are well aware that they are outwith nature and yet they have a probability which is not preposterous against the natural background. Thus we accept the mermaid, the satyr and the unicorn as 'probable creatures' but reject, say, the griffon, the sphinx and the minotaur. There is a dual reason for our choice. Firstly, the plausibility of actual form—there is an œsthetic fitness about the creatures which isolates them from mere freakishness; they possess beauty and dignity. And, secondly, we sense their symbolic significance; we are conscious that they were not born out of fancy but were expressive needs created by the imagination to emblem some inarticulate intuition of delight and desire with something of that awe which is inseparable from the beauty of the world and the mystery of life.

OCTOBER

WEDNESDAY 27
I would assert that not only is all creation symbolic of reality but that the endless variations and juxtapositions in, and of, phenomena are symbols, so that the eternal process of creation is bodied forth in an eternal change of symbol. Thus even the very limited area of life which is comprehended by the individual is far richer in symbolic content than is the comprehensive capabilities of the individual mind. One might almost—indeed one must—assume that so long as the individual retains and preserves his sensuous sensitivity he is able to apprehend new aspects of the truth no matter how restricted his environment. This again is but an illustration of the necessity for an assured differentiation between quality and quantity. In short we touch the truth even if only it be the chain which binds us.

NOVEMBER

TUESDAY 2

One cannot hope to isolate the true tap-root of nationalism, it goes down too deeply into the racial unconsciousness, but sometimes one can sense as if a portion of oneself has flowered upon the strength which rouses along a fibre of this root. One begins to be more conscious of the atavistic constitution of one's being; life still flows up from the loam of the past and stimulates the branches of one's blood. I feel this peculiarly in speech. English is *not* natural to me; and I use it 'consciously' even in conversation; it is always something of an effort for me to find my words; and not uncommonly I labour as if I were speaking in a foreign language. It is as if one had come out of the past with only a fragmentary memory of one's true tongue and yet this broken speech remained as rocks which disturb the flow of modern speech.

FRIDAY 5

Now that one can look back across a fair stretch of the years one is startled at the transitoriness of youth. My own, of course, was unnaturally short; and from this distance I am aware of only one year of which I can assert—'Then I knew fully what it was to be young.' That was my 18th year while yet the shadow of the war was unacknowledged. Then I was one of the fleetest at the Academy: one of the strongest: first in my year at most things: I was writing poetry: I was in love: I was popular both in the classroom and on the playing-field: I never reached this condition of living fullness again except in brief moments.

TUESDAY 9

CALEDONIA'S NEAR A CORP

Caledonia's near a corp;
Puir auld Caledonie:
Sckrog and skrank wi' English slorp
And English parsimony.

What can mak our Scotland hale:
What make her braw and bonnie?

Hamely brose and hamely kail,
Bannock and baup and sconie?

Wauk her wi' a Doric sang;
Dirl her wi' the dronie:
She'll come tae hersel' or lang
And gang as gleg as onie.

Gin she were hersel' aince mair
(And this is no a ronie)
A' the world wud wark to share
The rowth o' Caledonie.

THURSDAY 18

It would seem that if we are to retain the capabilities of
responding spontaneously to life—or of achieving what
might be called our second innocence—our faith must
be almost sheer faith unfortified by any doctrine that has
the possibility of being hardened into a rule. Nothing is
so withering to the tender tip of our sensitivity than the
acceptance of a ready-made code, for by so accepting we
prejudge experience and sacrifice the mystery for a measuring rod. Since there must be focal points from which
the spirit functions—centres of gravity, so to speak, which
enable the spirit to act constructively; rooting places from
which to grow—creeds are fundamental and cannot coerce
the spirit so long as we recognise that they are but symbols
of the truth.

DECEMBER

FRIDAY 17

How like a dream life can be with both the strangeness
and the inconsequence of a dream. How often, after the
departure of some visitors one looks about the emptied room
and thinks to the self, 'Now I have awakened.' Last night,
Corrie marched in with the collected poems of Kipling under
his arm. Little Stevens was already settled by the fire and
had disembosomed himself of the therapeutic gain which
had come to him from psychotherapy. The massive Corrie
acknowledged the young man's presence and no more—he
was too eager to begin his recital. On and on and on he

boomed out the galloping rhythms and the echoes had
scarcely died away when Stevens had to depart. Then I
was transported to the East and heard the imam calling from
his tower and I hoped that Corrie's big boots would leave
our fireplace intact. Now and then there was a muttering of
Malay words when the silence halted between us—Corrie
had lapsed back to Malaya without me. As he left he recalled
some mundane matter and asked for a 1½ *d.* stamp.

SUNDAY 26

Between 40–45, when a man has come to the middle of
his adult life, it would seem that he must gather up his
courage more wilfully, having left behind him the optimism
of youth. Now he looks life and himself fully in the face
and must go forward with no delusive fancies. At least so
it seems to myself who can hardly hope for a much longer
continuation of comparatively kindly days. Rather must I
anticipate a journey which will be more and more solitary,
more and more distressed, more and more burdensome. And
at this very hour of realisation I find my desire for sexual
completion more compelling than it has ever been; but then
are we not most fond, most tender, at the moment when we
must say good-bye?

CHAPTER NINE

— 1938 —

JANUARY

SUNDAY 16

We can never uncover the ultimate roots of our preferences and we may actually prefer one thing to another for quite different reasons from such as we offer. I myself, for example, love the blackbird more dearly than the thrush and for these reasons—but I am aware that another might confute them all. The blackbird seems to me to be the more masterly creation, and more cleanly bodied forth from the matrix of thought—fresh like a newly-shed chestnut. In comparison the thrush is something of a country cousin; there is a hint of the provincial about him—that handsome front is just a trifle 'glorious'; how perfect in comparison the blackbird's solitary bright bill against the body's darkness. Exuberance has become quintessential here—life poised like the sparkle on a wave-crest; life's joy culminated in a single gesture—the flirt of a tail-feather; and the magnanimity of life flowing in the rich simplicity of a song.

MONDAY 17

Vignettes.

1. Gordon Grant comes *in* with his increasing corpus sticking *out*; and with bluff wit remarks: 'It is either dropsy or twins.'

2. David Stevens sitting over his supper-plate groaning in spirit while he lifts an enormous piece of cake to his expectant jaws.

TUESDAY 25

In the evening a most uncommon and prolonged 'broadcast' of the aurora borealis: Robin's name literally acted out in the sky . . .

On the Anniversary of Burns' birthday, 1938,
when the whole sky, for many hours, was illuminated
by the northern lights

Lat a' you ranters at the clubs;
In print, in poopits, or in pubs;
Gir owre your gabblin for the nicht:
Nae dout the ha'penny-dips ye burn
About the haggis dae their turn—
But look! the lift is fu' o' licht.

FEBRUARY

SATURDAY 26

There are moments when the earth seems to have paused
in expectancy: we sense her as a presence—a living reality
whose hills and glades are but the garments which she wears.
Now the mind looks out on such a moment halted under a
dull sky. Stiff and dark the barren boughs stretch against
the greyness; the smoke goes up unbroken by the wind:
the sudden cry of a child ceases as quickly as if the air had
grown wholly unsubstantial. Life is withdrawn into itself,
brooding upon the verge of a fresh initiation: the very birds
turn on the bough in pantomimic silence. Only the steady
gleaming flames of the crocuses, compact against the chill
weather, have anticipated the earthy expectancy: to-morrow,
or perhaps the next day, we shall all be confiding to the self
that spring has indeed returned.

MARCH

SUNDAY 13

A robin has begun to build in one of the bird-boxes fixed
to the rose-bower—worked all yesterday 'from morn till
dewy eve' innocent of Sabbatical transgression: the Sabbath was made for the birds also and not the birds for
the Sabbath. . . . D. B. Low came in. Jawing. On Eve's
return from the Bible Class at 6.0, D. B. L. fetched in his

spaniel 'Bobby' from the car. The day which had begun
with intimations of wild life ended with exhibitions of tame
life. . . . Wholly domesticated creatures have no attraction
for me: nobility has gone out of them and their devotion
has ever a slavish taint. We are fascinated by the eagle and
the tiger not only in themselves but also because we see life
symbolised in them—life which we cannot seduce or bribe:
life which demands unconditional allegiance.

SUNDAY 27
Finished reading Murry's *Keats and Shakespeare*[1] again.
This work to me was, and still is, a critical masterpiece:
I can think of no other study—of this nature—carried
through so consistently and with so keen an awareness: it
is a classic of imaginative sensitivity. Murry's is the one contemporary mind—apart from D. H. Lawrence's—whose
'identity' (to apply Keats' own terminology) has 'pressed
itself' upon me. This has continued now for about a dozen
or more years—and seems likely to continue until the end.
In Murry I see a spiritual growth; and accordingly there
has been always an unpredictableness about him: and those
who have had preconceived notions of his development
have generally blamed him for failing to conform to their
surmisals. Hence his comparative isolation considering his
contemporary significance.

APRIL

SATURDAY 16
About 4.0 a Mr Fortey of Bath—'the only Englishman
who is a Scottish poet' so introduced himself. A biggish,
bald man of 65—with MSS. attached. Must have had a
touch of the sun, or something, poor chap: as a poet he
was quite assured that he was *forte*—and no doubt the rest
of us *pianissimo*; even unheard as well as unseen. Soon
he was performing—rather well—with his eyes 'heaved
up'; big eyes like his voice but dullish like his verse. Is
he a warning sent from heaven—a premonition that the
renaissance in Scots embodies an eccentricity which, in the

generous amplitude of life, has been granted a gesturing moment; but which by indulgence will degenerate into deathliness.

MAY

SATURDAY 14

Having again read Housman's *More Poems* one is forced to the conclusion that his philosophic attitude had been definitely exploited in his previous two collections; and his self-awareness is shown in limiting his work to these. Housman knew what he could do and knew that he couldn't keep on doing it indefinitely: his field was narrow and not rich enough to produce more than a strictly weeded-out harvest. How restricted it was may be shown by comparing his work with the range of the Scottish ballad. He was essentially a ballad-writer and has much of the starkness and a touch of the brutality: pathos is there, too, and bare irony—but the glory of life, the profound tenderness, the diablerie, and that other-worldness which is yet our own at some moment when beauty and terribleness have conjoined, lighting up a mood or scene as if by a steady luminacy of wildfire: these enter but fitfully into his work or not at all.

THURSDAY 19

Like all profound associations I cannot date when the unicorn began to impress itself upon me—but it was no doubt deepening by my early thirties when I was definitely turning to Scots and when I was experiencing a more limited physical life. Since then I can follow the growth of the symbol in two directions, the one towards a richer comprehensiveness and the other towards a subtler privacy. Thus from a purely Scottish emblem the creature has come to represent truth, reality, life under varying aspects but all manifesting the eternal nature of man's quest; always he is but holding the image in the pool of his mind: so the arts, philosophies and religions build up their cages round an ever elusive vision. The private identification has grown out of circumstance and an element of aloofness in my own nature: perhaps also, now, from the premonition that with the years I may find myself more and more alone.

JUNE

SUNDAY 12
What I admire in a woman is vitality; the languorous beauty or the intellectual type has a much less immediate appeal: and this I suppose is true for the majority of men. The flame of life which we look for primarily in masculine speculation we seek in the feminine presence; manifested by the lifting of the head, the grace of a gesture, the firmity of limb and breast. These, alas, still tempt me along the by-path of fancy and make me realise how difficult it is to free oneself wholly from the romanticism of adolescence: even as the soul maintains 'This is my necessity' the body answers 'I also have my need.' This vitality is not so common; but now and again we meet it. D. P. has it, so that it suddenly looks out from her eyes, sounds in her voice, and is seen even in her stillness. A glance or gesture is sufficient to declare its potentialities not only for gaiety, passion and generosity, but also for anger, abandonment and violence: it is in truth a flame of life to illuminate or to destroy.

JULY

MONDAY 11
How quietly we may grow into an assurance—tho' we may be deceiving the self; nevertheless when the growth is slow and the assurance comes as a surprise—like the presence of a flower which we knew had been maturing and yet by its display takes us unawares—we are prone to assume that our certainty is not altogether a self-deception. Thus I find that I now accept that some of my poems will live—not only for those in Scots but also in English. I now sense that a portion of experience, voiced in these lyrics, is rooted in reality, that in some small measure life flowers in them. Such an assumption, whatever its justification may be, is at least potent at the moment in the self—since it empties the

heart of concern for contemporary praise or blame: though one is made happy for the moment by a friendly salute.

SEPTEMBER

SUNDAY II

Listening-in—heard Barrie's *Mary Rose*. Much of it holds one but every now and then one is conscious of a falsity to experience; every now and then Barrie side-steps reality and betrays life. He is seduced by the sentimental. Might we not see in the theme of *Mary Rose* a symbol of life-betrayal: at the end she is freed from reality to enjoy her 'fairy-land'. The solution is childish—Mary Rose at the end has become a child but not in the Blakean sense: it is a lapse back not a winning through. In short, Barrie ever holds back from confronting tragedy full-faced.[2]

MONDAY I2

Even as we should approach life without any preconceived conditions so should we come to a work of art. But—having willingly submitted to the nature of the author's world—the condition of our sustained acceptance is that the author also conforms to the world within which his theme develops: this, of course, is especially so when he introduces us to a fanciful or supra-normal creation. In *Mary Rose*, for example, the supernatural element is assumed to be malignant and the human reaction is either to have nothing whatever to do with it or, having been drawn within its orbit, to oppose it: in other words, the situation is a tragic one. Yet at the end of the play Mary Rose is given over to this power irrevocably and the tragic issue is evaded. This solution is symptomatic of Barrie's refusal in all his work to grapple with the tragic reality and the consequence is always a betrayal of the dignity of man.

FRIDAY 23

To look upon the passage of the sun and the certain progression of the stars during the time of battle is not to be repulsed by the indifference of nature but to be admonished by the silent witnessing to the laws which, in their spiritual orientation, we have broken.3 As the light and the rain come down beyond all good and evil so come the exhortations of sun and stars offering the wisdom which is older than the mind of man. It is the blindness of our pride and our lust for power which shuts our aspiration within the boundaries of earth: yet the silent things of earth also proclaim the same wisdom—that nothing exists of itself and for itself, but that all are sustained by all. So vision looks through the semblance of reality to the life of life and takes assurance from the necessity of obedience which is the body of love.

SATURDAY 24

Sometimes we may wonder why the relationship of man and woman occupies so large a portion of life and art—but the reason is obvious enough. For the majority of folk the mutuality of sex is the one relationship which links them to life in vital partnership. Even at its nadir sex exemplifies the law of gain by reciprocity; even at its blindest there is acknowledgment of the beauty which is the image of reality. But in true love sex is the common ground whereon all may find the joy of creative experience. The other becomes a quintessential knowledge of life's loveliness, of life's demand for unconditional trust, of life's basic interdependence so that in the tangible we have a vision of the oneness of all things. And with the child the creative act of faith is come to fullness; in the child desire and life's need meet, and there both death and life meet and are indistinguishable.

OCTOBER

WEDNESDAY 5

What I shall never be able to evaluate, even if I possessed a far richer humankindliness, is the influence of these six hundred friendly visitations upon my solitude. I am well aware that I greatly undervalue them; though not so crassly insensitive to their formative potency as in time past or so selfishly blind to the goodwill which must prompt so many of them. But how well-nigh impossible to have maintained some sort of balance between the world of day and the private world of the self had not these friends come in from the busyness outside and by their presence elicited responses which had otherwise dwindled for lack of summoning. How we can deceive our self with thoughts and gratuitous imaginings of generosity; fanciful deeds of goodwill and courage; but our fellows come before us and so coming teach us that to become human one must co-operate with human beings; to become an individual one must accept the individuality of others.

WEDNESDAY 12

At a time when calamity appears to be unavoidable; when one is forced to accept that men are faced towards a major doom in which beauty and innocence will share the horrors of destruction; that is, at a time such as our own, when the destiny of civilisation has been entrusted to four representative men who are destitute of magnanimity and creative imagination4—then faith must set its feet upon the bare rock of a life-allegiance; against the knowledge of the destructive necessity must be balanced the indestructible trust that life is ever victorious. This is the fatalism of faith—that always the five just men shall be found and though the city perish, yet these, Abraham-wise, will emerge from disaster bearing in their bodies the promise of a new age; and in their memory the assurance that death is not only a barrier to life-betrayal but also a doorway to a fresh beginning.

SUNDAY 23

Prompted, in the main, by that numerical favouritism which I bestow on 9 I assume that the full cycle of human years is the square of 9 and thus I have now come half-circle. On this assumption it is far from flattering to admit that my epitaph at the moment would be: 'Here lies a man who could love only at a distance.' In the light of this admission to the self it becomes all the more needful that I keep a most watchful eye upon my protestations of trust in life and upon my philosophic assumption that necessity is the polarity of love. I know something of necessity but how little of love; and the easiest thing in the world is to evolve a metaphysic which is a buttress to one's own fallibility. The desires of the flesh, however tormenting, by their insistence bring us down from mere speculation to human interdependence: how easy to profess a metaphysical charity, how difficult to inherit that magnanimity of man which is found only when affection has grown into spontaneous response.

NOVEMBER

SUNDAY 13

The consciousness of failure which continually tormented Amiel resulted from his failure to recognise what manner of man he was; he halted from taking the final step of awareness which would have been the fully conscious acceptance of himself. He was in very truth secretly ashamed of the sensitivity which made him what he was because he could not reach a final decision about himself; in other words his intellect never wholly ratified the certainty of his feelings. Yet few, if any, have possessed a more experiencing nature than he; and if he was denied a corresponding comprehensive creative capability, his *Journal Intime* is the world's most profound exposition of the Keatsian quality. The one thing lacking was the capability of being content in the midst of his doubts—but his ὕβρις 'leaned to virtue's side': he was, if that be possible, a too-humble man; too diffident of his great gifts; too easily imposed upon by more extraverted minds. And yet had he been other than he was could there have been for legacy a *Journal Intime*?

MONDAY 21

Perhaps a man, such as myself, who cannot claim that he possesses a profound affection for his fellows and who is yet rarely left unvisited for a single day may assume that he at least provides an atmosphere in which men and women are at ease. 'In his presence even the reticent became confiding'—that were an epitaph not without tenderness; and to be worthy of it would be not to have wholly failed one's fellows. But if, in part, I seem to welcome my friends into such an atmosphere I cannot boast that I create it: the condition is given because I am what I am; namely, one who by nature has so little need to let myself overflow the private vessels of confession, my diaries, notebooks and verses: hence it is a normality in me that I should in turn become a vessel into which others pour themselves; and my response is this acceptance—though from time to time I also have my moments of 'expansion' and also my moments of confessional surfeit.

DECEMBER

FRIDAY 9

Like the giant of classical mythology poetry loses its potency when its contact with earth is meagre. In poetry the spiritual richness is determined by the depth, subtlety and multifariousness of sensation; out of the magnanimity of touch is born the generosity of expression. To be in touch has therefore a very tangible meaning for the poet; and the fruit of his achievement is ever a confession of how superficial or how deep are his roots in earth. Only by this unbroken contact with things, only by this alert mingling of sense and sensibility can his work maintain its symbolic wholeness, able to reflect a sun-bright sanity undistorted by the sentimentality of fancy or the barrenness of intellectuality. Poetry is like a woman who to be loved unconditionally must be loved both as a creature of flesh and of spirit, and so loved that both are as one in mutual recreativeness.

WEDNESDAY 28

Seeing a couple well-content with the little world about their home, their conversation circumscribed by the associations of their local busyness—their consciousness of the emergent future narrowed into the womb or the green tufts above the stubble-field, their sensitiveness of the mystery seemingly lost in the bustle of buying and selling, in the rattle of domestic pots and pans, in the hum of tittle-tattle and in the murmur of the machines: seeing such a couple—albeit they have the freedom to come or to go, albeit they have the mutuality of affection, albeit they have a centre of security, albeit they set out within their

limitations a purposive cycle which satisfies and leaves them
with a contented assurance—yet I know such an existence
were deathly to me and that the undefined, uncertain and
unreasonable life which is mine is my choice, tho' it may
seem to have been put upon me.

THURSDAY 29

It is the premonitory shadows which force the moment into
intensified brightness; and, since the coming year may hold
in its womb a crisis more decisive than that which is but
overpassed, we look out upon the ending year with the
consciousness that when again another year is at an end
we may remember this moment as the ending of a time.
Stillness is now in the air, and grass smoothly brightened
by the wintry sun. The bare rods of the apple trees glitter
as if varnished, the wings of the pecking crows shine darkly
like roughened metal. Lesser birds curve over the hedge
and alight with no sound—it is the quiet which assumes the
breathlessness of apprehension. In it we listen for children's
voices, the whistle of a boy, the sound of a hammer or of a
bell—these to be memories of a moment still lifted above
the triumph of the machines.

CHAPTER TEN

— 1939 —

JANUARY

SUNDAY 1

Waited up until 1.30 but Jim[1] did not come—must still be depressed *in profundis* even at this moment of *gloria in excelsis*. This estrangement, which I can hardly accept in seriousness, is yet significant of the incongruities which thrive out of faction. We all assume that our attitude is the one which will best assure the stability of social life; the best that is for the establishment of brotherhood—and yet, by focusing our vision too rigidly upon our own faith, we grow blind to the necessities of others and even at the very moment of our protestations of good-will we condemn those who are not pledged to our own peculiar trust. But if I can look upon Jim's withdrawal with no deep feeling either of loss or hurt—because I assume its temporariness and imbalance—yet it is symptomatic of the conflicting conditions of contemporary life and prophetic of the much more serious and separating circumstances which will be created if a time of battle should come.

SUNDAY 29[1]

* Are we appreciative enough of the generosity of youth? Raibeart Scouller's gesture of kindliness in coming from Glasgow to visit me, tho' one of those acts beyond assessment, is yet on a basis of computation an ample demonstration of youthful good-heartedness. He is but 21 and

---

[1]Entries indicated by a * for the years 1939 and 1940 are from Soutar's *Common-Day Book*.

cannot have a wage capable of keeping him in more than necessities—yet his train-fare must have cost him something like 12 shillings. Had I been a person of assured status and with the reputation of a profound conversationalist such a journey were explicable perhaps—but as things are it is a fine tribute to the large-heartedness of youth; to that imaginative liberality which endows others with greater attributes than they possess; nor is this gratuity an elevated form of deception but is congruent to a magnanimous nature which is conscious of the rich potentiality of man. There is a timorous meanness in the fear of being deceived—and it is by expecting great things from our fellows that we retain a humankindliness that remains unembittered even by deception.

MONDAY 30

* There was a man burning brushwood just beyond our hedge and I enjoyed watching the flames which sometimes spired up more than fifteen feet. How fitting a symbol of life is the energetic leap and dart of a flame. Now lowered as if gathering strength for the exultant upsurge; now, as it were, springing invisibly into the air to manifest itself like a banner instantaneously flaunting out of nothingness; now for a moment poised in tremulous evanescence upon a fragment of silence. Here life reveals itself—as a process of creation out of destruction, the phoenix sign of the exuberance that rises iridescent out of death. The movement however wavering and relapsing is accumulatively an ascent into glory, a triumph over bonds and corporality, and yet made real by dependence upon the martyrdom of matter. On gazing upon the intensity of a great flame we are riven out of our self, carried up into the swirl of light and scattered in exultation to the four corners of the sky; emptied of our desire to hoard or to be assured. The movement of the sea also empties us; it also is a major symbol of life but its aspect even as its spiritual nature is altogether different. In the sea we stare upon the resolution of the many and the one, the unison of diversity, the stability of flux. The sea liberates us by filling us with itself; we are stilled by its monotony which is never monotonous, we are imperceptibly

surcharged by its tide; we are lost, we are drowned, we are one with the eternal murmur—which we no longer hear.

FEBRUARY

TUESDAY 7
Ah! those women of the soulful sort—always busied with good works, always leading on the conversation into edifying and improving highways, always fluttering up into the more rarified strata of the spiritual atmosphere; always enthusing and enthusing and enthusing. Somehow, though we feel that their earnestness is praiseworthy and that their intentions are kindly and well-meant—yet they smother our response: perhaps in seeking prematurely to be angels they have unwittingly destroyed their womanhood. Certainly the norm of this type is generally an attenuated spinster or a childless wife; and the pardoxical effect upon us of their spiritual preoccupation is to make us more and more hypercritical of their sensuous deficiencies: the balance has been lost and we resent the highfalutin disregard of the flesh, even as we are bored by the antipodal type who is all bosom and thighs and mindless, girlish laughter.

WEDNESDAY 8
* Helen Thomas. It was an exhilarating coincidence that my re-reading of H. T.'s *As It Was* should follow just after I had made my diary entry on the 'spiritual' type of woman suggested by Mrs. Overy. No poet of any worth envies the gift of another; even as no human being of any worth desires to be another; but I am certain that many men consider that Thomas was most fortunate in having so rare a woman for his wife and would that their lot could be so apportioned. Thomas himself has left no poem more lovely than this story of their love in which the writer by the rare normality of her womanhood assumes a beauty so inextricably compounded of flesh and spirit that for comparison we must go to the pages of Shakespeare.

TUESDAY 14
We may borrow most appropriately Lamb's excellent phrase and speak about 'the divine plain face' of Burns' muse.

How misconceptual to surmise that because Burns' poetry
is lacking in speculation it is not profound; its profundity
is not comprehensive as Shakespeare's or Dante's; it is
hemispherical compared with their complete world; but in
its sensuous province it is full-ranging. The excellence of
Burns is in his power of recreating common emotion which
is possible only by that direct simplicity attainable when
the poet is a man of great magnanimity and spontaneous
responsiveness. What distorts many a genius, namely his
assumption of difference, or isolation and peculiarity,
was overborne in Burns by what we might term his
consciousness of the divine commonalty of human-nature.
It is this awareness which is so desperately needed in
modern literature when, with talk enough of classlessness
and brotherhood, we endure the arrogance of intellectuality
and the brutality of force.

   * Our normal response to natural phenomena is œsthetic
and not analytic—that is to say that we are conscious
of the generalities and not the particularities and this
is accountable for our normal ignorance of detail. For
example, we could rarely tell how many petals make up
certain common flowers; whether a bird when scratching
its head lifts its leg over or under the wing; whether an ox's
horns are before or behind its ears; and which birds hop
and which run. The majority of us, too, are hazy as regards
the colour of our friends' eyes—and this instance illustrates
not only our premise but also wherein the loveliness of an
eye resides: actually in the eye itself hardly at all excepting
by size and clarity; otherwise it is the formation of the
lids, its general setting which determines so much of its
expression, and also the proportioning of the face as a
whole with especial reference to the shape of the nose and
eyebrow.

MARCH

FRIDAY 17
* Corrie as a being is also natural enough, yet has this
element of queerness about him which, in relation to

myself, is manifested by plundering me of cigarettes. I
have usually a box on the mantelpiece for my friends, apart
from my own supply, and it is amusing to see Corrie's eyes
turn to the mantelpiece immediately after the handshaking.
If I omit to tell him at once to help himself one can notice
that he is on edge to be at the box, and sometimes he hasn't
the patience to wait for the invitation. One day on lifting
the box immediately after entering (I not being smoking
at the time) he found it empty and, having looked inside
for a moment or two as if incomprehendingly turned to me
with a hand out as a dumb solicitation. The half-apologetic,
half-expectant look on his face reminded me of that on a
dog who has had quite enough biscuits but would like
one more. As he smokes 3 cigs to my 1 this dumb-show
procedure continued for quite a while until he varied its
monotony by intimating that he'd try the next one in
his pipe. His record so far for a visitation has been 10
cigarettes, the final one pocketed to smoke on his journey
home.

APRIL

MONDAY 17

Now and then one is surprised at the insensitivity of a
critic of quality—as if an inexplicable hiatus were manifested in the landscape of his appreciation; a total blank
where one had anticipated a colourful illumination. Such
a shocked surprise came to me the other day on opening
T. F. Henderson's book on *Scottish Vernacular Literature*
to find out what he had to say by way of comment on
Hume's 'The Day Estivall'. I had just been reading this
poem again—a poem to which I am often persuaded to
return when prompted by a lovely day—and having its
freshness so vividly in my mind it was all the more
astonishing to be confronted by Henderson's contemptuous
aside: ' . . . "The Day Estivall", if absurdly prosaic, is
occasionally picturesque.' To me Hume—by the simplicity
of his style, the total elimination of metaphysical adum-
bration, the quiet undertone of praise and worship, the

contentedness to be an eye and ear peacefully receptive to the richness of the earth and sky and the busyness of man as an integral movement across the landscape—has recreated with quintessential fidelity that mood which dominates the mind grown pacific in the presence of nature's serene fruition.

WEDNESDAY 19

Though the desire for women troubles the body and the mind I am yet glad that desire is still so alive in me for its death would be ominous of creative moribundity. The lesser desires of sense rarely disturb me now—as if the loveliness of earth had become quintessential in women; as if in them were now summated those other sensations which quicken the whole being as one enters a wood, or lies upon a hillside, or stares across the sea. We gather the world into the compass of our speculation; and when our sensuous scope is small we can keep contact with the world only by quintessential symbol—so, in large measure unconsciously, the urge to retain living contact has intensified for me the significance of the commonplace. And since our contact with life has a trinal quality—natural, human, and metaphysical—there are for me three dominant images which are as doors into fuller life; and these are woman, tree and the unicorn.

SATURDAY 22

CONTRAST

Beneath the afternoon sun
Two pale-faced girls in black
Are carrying daffodils into the cemetery.
Overheard on the bough of a sycamore
The dark bird with the yellow beak
Sings; a fountain mouth of melody
Under whose flood the drowned faces
Drift on in silence.
The sky serene, remote;
With a handful of snow-bright cloud
Scattered and half-dissolving in froth.
The bird sings on:

The pale-faced girls in black
Move among the pale stones;
Over them the clear stillness of the afternoon:
Under them the dark silence of the cemetery.

MAY

THURSDAY 18

* Frank H. Fortey the one and only English Scottish Bard called with tartan tie but without portfolio. Within five minutes he had begun the recital announcing each poem as if from print, and by Fortey *in cathedra poetæ*, thus:—'Bonnie Scotland' composed in Glen Tootlum on April 19th 1938 by Frank H. Fortey of Bath. Fortey is a heavy man of 65 who seems heavier than he is by a large shapeless sort of head, and a pallidity which suggests that he is all fat and no beef. As he continues to declaim on and on, one begins to have the feeling that he is spouting a rarefied oileaginousness and that the room is slowly filling with it. The passions which he is so confident that his poetry evokes pass before the eye of fancy as a procession of fatty degenerates—mirth has a paunch too heavy for shaking, pity weeps greasy tears, and fondness sighs with a triple chin. Only his voice at moments protests, rising into a high, wavering and half-strangulated falsetto to hover tremulously for a little above the unctuous ooze of the rhythm before falling again to be engulfed.

JUNE

MONDAY 19

* At the distance in this dull light the underside of the sycamore leaves when blown up by the wind looks like grey canvas. Now indeed I stare for an instant on a 'plain' tree—a branching pole stuck all over with pieces of stiffly flapping cloth.

WEDNESDAY 21

* IN MEMORIAM

There was a Scots poet wha had a nostalgia
For the drone o' his pipe in praise o' his ain verse:
And ae wintry nicht I gat the neuralgia
As I thol'd his dringlin drant—and thocht o' my hearse.

Haud on! haud on! that's no the end o' my story
Though I was shair and eneuch o' whaur and what was hell;
But Lod! I had only been through purgatory
As I kent owre weel whan I gat the verse itsel'.

SATURDAY 24
* Just beyond my window there is a large, full-blown, pink
rose at the top of a long stalk. As I was looking out this
evening a sparrow glided down through the air and settled
on the rose as if it had been a nest. It did not remain
for more than a minute, nor did it actually nestle—and I
surmise it was hunting for aphides which are not plentiful
this season. I was surprised to note how easily the long stem
bore the additional weight as if the bird were no heavier than
a flower. Indeed after the sparrow had gone the rose seemed
in no way to have been ruffled.

SUNDAY 25
* When Mr Reeves returned to my room this evening after
supper he was wearing horn-rimmed spectacles—my first
introduction to them. As he settled himself, I said: 'You
have your glasses on now, I see,' and added some joky
remarks about having to don spectacles in order to enhance
the proportions of the contents of his plate—both culinary
and offertorial. Now completely settled he placed the tips
of his fingers together and, having assumed an aspect of
gravity, began to speak in a tone of benedictory quiescence.
'I always put on my glasses when having a meal—but I
cannot explain why I do so. This has been my custom for
many years now; yet it was but lately that my wife, during
a supper shared with friends, said abruptly to me: "Daddy!
why do you wear your glasses at meal times?" I answered:
"For years now, as you must have noticed, Mother, I have

worn my spectacles on such occasions—and I wonder that
you should ask me why at this moment." Later when by
ourselves I reproached her gently, and enlightened her that
this would continue to be my custom, and that I could not
explain why I do so and will do so.' Perhaps I, too, by
this confession was gently reproached and mysteriously
enlightened.

JULY

TUESDAY 11

* In a restricted environment the most ordinary things
acquire a power of distraction which would seem fantastic in
more normal circumstances. Thus should the glint of a bird
alighting on the green or the glimpse of a butterfly make
me conscious of their proximity, I follow their movements
for some time as if it were of importance to know what they
should do next. In like manner, with something of ritualistic
observance, I lay aside whatever I may be doing each Friday
morning, and for a quarter of an hour or so watch Jenny
cleaning the windows. Since I can see my visitors only in
part, due to my position in bed, she has come to embody
the human form in action; and although diminutive, and
but ordinary in shape, not without neatness; so that now
and then I catch momentary gestures of beauty in the
turn of the body or the slope of a limb. Fortunately she
never betrays by a gesture of self-consciousness that she
has any thought of being watched—otherwise my preoccupation would assume, if persisted in, a less pardonable
Tom-peepery.

SUNDAY 30

I am not blind, of course, to the fact that my reiterated
insistence that man is superior to his circumstances is as
an exhortation to myself to be ready to live out my own
assertion when the genialities of my environment may be no
more. Then the limitations and dependence, which at the
present are made easily endurable by affection and financial
security, shall become (by the loss either of mutuality
or means) burdens to be borne in full consciousness of

their restrictions and irksome necessities. However one may day-dream upon the possibility of a mutual affection capable of surmounting the irrevocabilities of fact—it is the premonitions of fact which have to be faced; and these would advise me to prepare for an ever-increasing challenge from circumstance, and a solitariness mitigated only by concentrating upon such creative efforts as I can accomplish and by the qualified communion of friendship.

AUGUST

THURSDAY 31

Learned from the air this morning (Sep. 1st) that Germany had invaded Poland at dawn—already many cities are suffering bombardment; the first bomb fell among civilians hours ago. Now we await our own evacuees and the intimation that the first bomb has fallen upon London. The greatest catastrophe which has erupted in the world is already a fact although the oncoming surge of it has not as yet broken over us. Outside in the overcast day, the familiar sounds rise up through the quiet. Children are at play nearby, a tradesman's bell is ringing, someone rattles a pail. And in the garden the autumnal beauty still lingers, halted at this hour in stillness—scarcely a leaf moves on the sycamore tree, under the dark green of the hawthorn are still the blue and yellow blooms, a bird skims silently across the smooth stretch of grass. The peace which we have broken so barbarously abides here for yet another day.

SEPTEMBER

FRIDAY 1

* Jenny had just started to clean my window when the 10.30 a.m. news-bulletin began intimating that Germany had invaded Poland. Mother passed on the news to Jenny who on returning to her window-cleaning exhibited such an increased acceleration that she was done in less than half her normal time. With a like exuberance she tackled the summer-house windows; dashing up and down the

steps, and now and then sticking out her chest like a belligerent bantam. Evelyn remarked in the evening that the public-houses were crowded with young fellows, and numerous militia-men rolling along the streets. My own recollection of a personal reaction prompted by a similar mood takes me back to June 1916. On the afternoon when the report of Kitchener's death was made public I was crossing from the Academy to the North Inch where, on a strip of grass bordering the path to the left of the old cannon, a number of senior boys were practising putting the weight in preparation for the approaching sports. Before I had joined them somebody informed me that Kitchener had been drowned. This bit of news immediately galvanized me into a mindless exuberance, and I instantly set off towards the potential athletes leaping and running and shouting, 'Hurrah! Kitchener's dead!' Then on joining the staring party I picked up the weight and gave it a mighty heave outdistancing all the previous throws. I suppose the unconscious thought expressing itself in such a display of animal boisterousness is: 'Look, Death, look; here is somebody alive and very much alive.'

MONDAY 4
* A sad and strange experience this morning. Just before five o'clock while it was yet very dark I was awakened by the ringing of our front-door bell—followed by rappings on the door and the flashing of a lantern into the hall. I had to shout three or four times before Evelyn heard me and awoke the folks. As I had surmised it was a policeman and with him was Lizette Mackenzie's friend Dorothy Campbell to inform us that Lizette had been in a deranged condition for a week; and that some little time ago she had won free from her room by leaping out of the window. They had expected to find her here as she had asserted, on being denied money to go to Iona, that she'd get it from me. Dorothy and the policeman had just gone when I heard the sound of a dull blow on my window. When my father peered out at the corner of the blind, there was Lizette with her hair on her shoulders and some flowers in her hand. He phoned the police to let them know that she had been found and then

went to the little summer-house door, at which Lizette was
now quietly standing. On opening the door, she said: 'God
has sent me with a message for Willie;' so she was brought
to me and we were left alone. She came over to me like a
tranced thing with the flowers in her left hand, and when
beside me took my right hand in hers. Then she looked up
to pray and said: 'Father, give me the words.' After a pause,
during which she seemed to be straining to make contact
with the unseen, she began to speak slowly and somewhat
haltingly, but quietly: 'Go to Murry (meaning Middleton
Murry) and tell him to go to Iona:' 'You can rise up:'
'Say, God, make me well:' so I said it: and continuing
as if deeper entranced she said: 'God, make me well and
save my soul from hell:" Jesus is married now:' 'I am
Christ in female form:' Between the pauses, it was with
difficulty that I refrained from uttering commonplaces such
as 'Won't you have a cup of tea?' and 'I hope your mother
is keeping well,' etc.: no doubt with some faint expectation
of bringing back sanity into the scene. Now she lifted up
her little bouquet which contained a single sycamore leaf,
a spray of yellow calceolarias and a yellow rose. 'The rose
the symbol of immortality:' 'The sycamore the symbol of
immortality:' 'You can rise up, now:' 'I shan't watch you.'
So saying she moved slowly to the door, stood there for a
few seconds, and having switched off the light went out to
the hall where the folks were waiting. Due no doubt to an
automatic relaxation from tension I felt my muscles ease,
and just to make certain that no miracle had been achieved
I attempted to bend my back and my legs, then I switched
on the light and waited. Lizette by this time was in the
bathroom putting up her hair—about the only concession
to propriety possible for her, as the flimsy skirt which she
had slipped over her nightdress had been ripped from hem
to thigh when climbing neighbouring hedges to reach our
garden. Before her toilette was completed, Dorothy arrived
at the door with two attendant constables and a police-car,
and it was arranged that when Dorothy and Lizette had
walked so far they would be overtaken by the constables
as if by chance and offered a lift home. Before leaving,
Lizette came into my room again already looking as if a

burden of necessity had been lifted off her. She gave no
sign of disappointment upon seeing me still in bed; and
after a moment's hesitation asked if I'd give her money
to go to Iona. I answered that I'd have to get it myself
first, and would have arranged about it before her return
later in the day. This satisfied her, and she said good-bye
brightly enough answering my 'Take care of yourself' with
a little smile and the words 'But I haven't any self.' She
was in some pain, however, as her half-leap half-fall had
been from a second storey window and her back had been
bruised. When the house was again quiet one could have
been persuaded that the whole episode had been enacted
in a dream-world, if the lingering fragrance of the rose had
not remained in the room to affirm its reality.

TUESDAY 19

To adopt a pacifist attitude were hypocritical presumptuous-
ness if one believed that the life of man was a self-contained
process; it is only out of the conviction that the activities
of humanity are centred in cosmic purpose and meaningful
when obedient to living law that pacifism is freed from
false-assumption. It is not that the pacifist is more human or
more magnanimous than his fellows but that he has become
more conscious of the nature of reality, and accordingly
able to act with full awareness of the need of the hour.
He is not blind to his dependence upon the community
but he is as deeply sensible of the gifted nature of life and
that his ultimate allegiance is to the source. His strength
is not his own but maintained by his assurance of life's
pervading presence, essential in his trust, and manifested
daily in nature and in the many unrecorded words and acts
of goodwill which he partakes from his common mingling
with men.

THURSDAY 28

* The blackbird is indeed a 'stream-lined' beauty, and in
movement always a delight to watch. The other day one
had a most exhilarating flirtation with a dead leaf which it
hunted around for quite a while. I noted that it sometimes
whirled it into the air with a sudden wing-beat, but I am

not certain whether this was intentional or whether it just happened by chance as the bird scurried about.

This morning a small brown and white cat climbed into the sycamore tree on the prowl for birds. Now and then a glint of white appeared among the leaves but its presence was otherwise betrayed only by the waving of a branch in the almost windless air. When Jenny went up to fill the bird-bath and scatter crumbs she was attracted by the uncommonly lively leafage but did not approach to discover the cause. I need hardly say that the birds avoided the tempting spread on the green so long as the sycamore veiled their enemy. As I continued to watch I saw an outer branch become excessively agitated, and a few leaves fell prematurely. Then a couple of feline hind-legs swung into view clawing helplessly—and after a moment or two of suspense (and suspension), the little cat tumbled down amongst the shrubs.

OCTOBER

TUESDAY 3
* During a conversation which Mr McMorris had shared lately with a certain Mrs B—(the wife of a Kirkcaldy undertaker) the lady confided that her husband had been advised to take in an enormous stock of timber so that he should be able to cope with the mortality of air-raids; a possible enough eventuality in a town on the Forth. Mr Mac commented that this must have entailed a big expenditure; and concluded: 'I suppose it would mean a loss if all that stuff were left on his hands.' 'O! yes:' innocently answered the good lady: 'It would be a dead loss.'

SUNDAY 15

* EPITAPH

Here lies an idiot, Tom Fyfe,
Who had been happy all his life.

FRIDAY 20
This was Little Dunning day—but everybody seems to have forgotten its pastime gaiety when the High Street was lined all along both pavements with stalls displaying innumerable particoloured wares. And especially heartening to the eye of a boy were the many sweetie-stalls so overburdened—with sugar pigs, pink-hearts, barber-pole sticks, and confections of every shape and stain—that one marvelled to see the frail structures of wood bearing up under so wondrous a weight of delight. My affection for this day of thronging sweetmeats and ruddy-faced country-folk is interwoven by association with my recovery from a serious illness, the nature of which I was never very clear about, tho' I am aware that it began with a severe chill in the kidneys and reached a crisis in a day of delirium terminated by a profuse bleeding at the nose. It was on a Little Dunning anniversary that I first ventured out again, extra thin about the legs and somewhat awed by admonitions not to run or exert myself. So my re-entry into the living day synchronised with this local manifestation of bustle and laughing crowds and the coloured invitations to eat and be merry.

SUNDAY 29
* A month ago I made a note upon the blackbird's flirtation with the dead leaves. Yesterday I happened to look up from writing just in time to observe another—or perhaps the same bird—amusing himself among the apple-leaves fallen near the rockery hawthorn. This time, however, the procedure was different. The bird would peck over a leaf or two and then remain in his place with wings vibrating rapidly. My only explanation so far is that he was endeavouring to attract his partner, which may have been beyond my range of vision; for it is rather fantastic to assume that his wing-beating was an effort to raise up any ephemera that might be about the leaves. In any case I did not see him peck as if feeding—all such dabbings were confined to the throwing over of the leaves.

The little cat still frequents the sycamore tree although not a leaf now flutters on it. It is, nevertheless, an approach to the higher reaches of the hedge which is still fairly screened. Yet I saw the prowler crawl out on a barren branch and once again lose his balance; bumping down to earth after a few moments of airy clutching.

NOVEMBER

SUNDAY 12
* I suppose my introduction to verse was by the riddle—the Scots riddle[2] which bairns used to exchange: 'The wee, wee man in the reid reid coat': 'It hings high, it roars sair,' etc. I must confess a vulgar affection for the following:—

> I gaed up atween two mountains,
> I heard a muckle rair:
> I listened, and I listened,
> But I heard nae mair.

A weaker next of kin went as follows:

> A riddle a riddle, as I suppose,
> Twa sonsy chouks that wanted a nose.

MONDAY 13
Listened in to the trial scene from *St Joan* which is an epitome of Shaw's excellencies and limitations. The masterly control of dramatic dialogue, the irony, wit and balanced tension are all there, but when the moment for imaginative consummation arrives, Shaw fails. And his failure is as Barrie's failure, though for a different reason; is indeed the failure of a generation—namely to be true to the tragic vision; to accept the ultimate desolation of the tragic moment and by acceptance behold its consummated beauty and suffering. Shaw comes so near such an acceptance, within a word of it, one might say: for Joan had merely to utter the equivalent of Job's cry: 'Though he slay me, yet will I trust.' But the reality was lost for a literary device—a prolongation of suspense when the cry of human faith should have vindicated the eternal silence. Joan's final utterance is accordingly bathetic—sentimental commonplaces: and by the incontrovertible laws of life she who was capable of supreme spiritual isolation now fears a prison. Shaw has made her death not a martyrdom but an escape.

SUNDAY 26

THE SOLITARY PLACE

As through the wilderness he gaed
The stanes spak oot to speer his need:
'The mercy o' the world,' he said.

Rocks in their pity cried: 'What pack
O' naethingness boos doun your back?'
'The mercy o' the world, alack.'

Atween his tatters blench'd the bane:
Frae ilka airt wail'd the cauld win':
'The mercy o' the warld blaws in.'

And through the hollow o' his hand
He watch'd the sinderin drift o' sand:
A lane man in a lanely land.

DECEMBER

SUNDAY 3
* Marjorie Tod brought in her little sister Enid to see me—a
serious and pretty child of 10 or so. Being a poetess with
eight poems already in her notebook she wished to have
a look at me, and that I might have a look at her poems.
Why is it that so many sensitive children are fragile—are
their bodies also vulnerable to the touch of earth as their
minds to earthly beauty? How sensitive a child may be is not
easy to assess, since in childhood we are not self-conscious
about our suffering or joy—yet there is no doubt that our
impressions then go deep and tinge all our subsequent
days. Illness and the contempt of her companions for
her poetry-making (which Evelyn confided) have already
begun to teach Enid something of solitariness, and behind
her serious face will be a knowledge of which she is unaware.
As I have not yet seen her poems I cannot say how many
may reflect but a natural joy in loveliness or if any reveal
the unconscious need for understanding.

CHAPTER ELEVEN

— 1940 —

JANUARY

SATURDAY 6
*One of my lesser presumptions is to talk about current films as if I had seen them; and now it would seem that my persistence has so overborne the incongruity that the majority of my friends have become insensitive to the fact that I have not seen a film for more than fifteen years.

MARCH

FRIDAY I
* The Rev John Strathern returned with unexpected promptitude this afternoon (2nd) considering our heated argument of the 22nd. He had been burying a faithful parishioner and perhaps by association thought it appropriate to come in and bury whatever animosity might remain between us. As customary he brought a volume from which to give me a reading—and I suspect that his choice was not without premeditation. It was a collection of sermons by an Archbishop Church of Westminster, and for our mutual (?) consideration Mess John selected one upon the virtues of Christian forgiveness in the sharing of which I was no doubt both rebuked and restituted.

Just before leaving, John remarked: 'What colossal sums are now being spent upon this war,' then added naïvely, 'And nothing done on the Western front.' I had to laugh aloud at this implication that we were not getting our money's worth—and the divine himself joined in; but whether he recognised the theatrical incongruity of his aside I can't say.

SATURDAY 9
*A piece of asphalt had been left by the workmen, on the flower-border which skirts our side-path, and on lifting it up my father broke off the tip of a lily which had pierced into the covering fragment.

This evening there were half a dozen day-flies dancing outside my window—touched into life by the lightest fingering of the sun. How humiliating all the boasts and bombardments of international force when viewed against the natural operation of life's creative potency.

APRIL

TUESDAY 30
In an age such as ours can the poet hope to achieve more than a fragmentary utterance since his obligation is to be true to his time; since indeed the integrity of his naming is assured by his obedience to the hour, and his voice the voice of his contemporaries both in their faith and faithlessness, in their victories and defeats, in their satisfactions and sufferings. And since we are a generation in conflict the tension of struggle will be present in the poetry, an element both of frustration and strength, for the very flaws of necessity will be a testament to truth. And this faithfulness to the moment will have its own harmony for it will disclose not only the moment in its nakedness but in its relationship to life; nothing is meaningless save in isolation. If therefore in the tumultuous darkness of our day the poet can but peer in readiness for the visionary glimpses; if in other words his utterance will be mainly lyrical—the compulsion which is upon him will give magnitude to the momentary and purge it of personal concernment.

JUNE

TUESDAY 4
It is inevitable that with the prolongation of warfare the writer who has given his allegiance to pacifism should

experience with increasing intensity the constriction upon
creative effort. Unable to share in the patriotic fervour he
is thereby self-excommunicated from the manifold tensions
of battle which produce an emotional ferment, impure and
febrific, but nevertheless procreative. But not only is he
deprived of this general passion, he is also excluded from
general mutuality; and with the growing concentration of
the former he becomes more and more conscious of his
loss of the latter. His attitude, at first condoned, in time
promotes an ever-deepening antagonism, and with it the
necessity of a more and more conscientious watchfulness
in himself, lest his ostracism betray him into bitter or
sanctimonious response. Nor, being a man among men
and a poet of their tragic moment, can he find in nature
a substitute communion; since his vision, which must
look steadfastly on the conflict to see beyond it, retains
its images of strife even when turned upon the loveliness
of the natural day.

FRIDAY 28

Bill Mackenzie appeared unexpectedly this forenoon—has
been transferred to Leslie: certain troops being concentrated in Fife, as the Germans may attempt a landing
between the Forth and Tay. Bill looking very well; slimmer
and deeply sun-burned. Had got away from the Dunkirk
dunes in comparative safety—and was surprised that the
Germans hadn't bombed them more violently. However he
had been near enough death to retain a certain look in the
eyes which is undefinable—a kind of impersonal glance that
shows itself now and then.

JULY

THURSDAY 4

Finished reading *Anarcho-Syndicalism* by Rudolph Roeber.
This is my introduction to Anarchism and I find that
there is something in its basic recognition of the living
struggle of the people which especially appeals to me.
It has an element of humanness which seems lacking
in Marx-Leninism, but at present I am not qualified to

compare and contrast the two. It would appear from the contemporary development of events that we shall pass into some kind of totalitarianism—but our ultimate escape from bureaucracy might well be thr' some anarchistic movement. I sense that the character of the Scottish people, and probably the British as a whole, is more disposed to a decentralised form of government than to the acceptance of any kind of state-control however communal its intentions. Our symbol of efficiency is not the machine but the living human body; and a healthy body is one in which instinct and the will interact mutually.

MONDAY 29
Tom Scott[1] came in bringing a typed copy of his lengthy poem, 'On my 21st Birthday'. Much of this modern verse is unintelligible to me—and, naturally, much of this particular sample of it is too intimate in incident for general understanding. Scott also brought a couple of poems by his pal George Fraser.[2] There is a Ninetyish quality about the verse of these young moderns—but with a difference; the self-conscious daring is not in the carnality but in the technique: this gives their poetry a hardness which cuts through sentimentality but also shears away something of humankindness.

AUGUST

SATURDAY 3
Jennie in emancipated mood this forenoon dashing about at her window-cleaning with no stockings on: sometimes the glimpse of a free, young body gives me a sudden, hollow feeling in the pit of my stomach.

FRIDAY 16
This drifting into day-dream which is so dangerous; this ranging through unreality which is so negative; and which by the prolongation of circumscription becomes more and more liable: a bordering land into which one has wandered by a single side-step. And the phantoms which beckon most persistently are in the shapes of women—since that which

we would touch and cannot becomes the more desirable. And it is here that to follow the dream is to degenerate desire; to chase the image of creative joy and gather only the weeds of self-pity; sickly fondness, corruptive regret. The desire cannot be annulled—and it were deathly to wish it away, for it rouses from the core of creation and is the carnal sign of exuberant potentiality. It is therefore well that the shapes of living women delight even by tormenting: only the pursuit of their phantasms betrays the blood.

THURSDAY 22

I surmise that these times of lassitude, which I have experienced now and then since the beginning of hostilities, are fairly general during warfare. They are not physical in origin but come from an undifferentiated consciousness of the waste, futility and blind forcefulness operating all about one. The chill shade of deathliness which is over the world touches the very quick of our individual being; and at certain moments this feeling which insidiously pervades the mind reacts upon the blood. It is in desperate opposition to this mood of disintegration that the flesh grows more desireful of contact; and the increased carnality which is ever associated with warfare is not explicable merely as part of the general licence, but is prompted by the urge to attest the triumph of life even in the midst of death and destruction.

SEPTEMBER

MONDAY 9

MORTALITY

We winter, like a tree
Bared ablow the rime,
And dee monie a time
Afore we dee.

Oot o' cauld care and grief
Joy fleurs the mair free,
Sin getherin death maun gie
His hairst to life.

Aye look ayont the day;
And yet haud it dear
As it were your hindmaist care
Or hindmaist joy.

FRIDAY 20

Apart from writing the 'whigmaleerie' on the previous page ['The Three Worthies'], and some other odds and ends, I gave up yesterday to reading. In the afternoon I finished *Dialectical Materialism*, by David Guest—a promising young philosopher killed in the Spanish War. I find that my own conception of the relationship between love and necessity has much in common with Marx's philosophy and I hope to be able to resolve them both. As a contrast to Guest's book I read, in the latter part of the day, T. S. Eliot's essay, *The Idea of a Christian Society*. Eliot has an aristocratic clarity of style but dry in the mouth, and if it keeps the mind alert it rarely warms the heart; the quality is fine but lacks fullness; and we savour him in sips never in a mouthful.

OCTOBER

FRIDAY 11

Finished reading *The Scots Literary Tradition* by John Speirs—a capable little study within its limits, and comes near enough the truth in its analysis of the frustration which contemporary Scottish poets inherit. The linguistic dilemma confronting the Scottish writer is a peculiar epiphenomenon of the social impasse which is now general; and the fact that the ballad is the most stimulating source of inspiration for the modern writer in Scots manifests the social implications of the vernacular revival: it is symptomatic of our need and our desire to recreate a true community. . . . Alex Galloway[3] called: rather an amusing incident. Alex confessed that he could not rightly understand my poem, 'The Mystery', in the current number of *The Adelphi*; and on attempting to analyse it I discovered that it couldn't be done—so we left it wholly justified to its title.

MONDAY 14

A Douglas Young[4] introduced himself about 11 o'clock this morning—an exceedingly tall fellow with a shovel-beard—his leanness, longness and fringiness gave one the initial impression of a BBC announcer who had partially metamorphosed into an aerial: a fluent talker with a lectorial style: didn't just get his wave-length.

SATURDAY 19

The engines of the water-works continue to be partially cloggit and the water still something of a floody blux [sic]; but feelings of discomfort in the back nothing much.

CONFIDENTIAL

'You're no sae merry, my auld mill-wheel,'
Says I to my hert this mornin:
'What's garin ye boggle as ye breel
And taigle at ilka turnin?'

'Ye needna gang far to find the faut
That maks me wobble and wavel;
The race is nae langer at the trot
But cloggit wi' sand and gravel.'

[Written after a bout of renal colic due to stones.]

DECEMBER

FRIDAY 13

Mrs Stirling called and jawed on for a while—the usual chronicle of relatives who were born, married and died: yet in what other soil can comedy and tragedy root?

CHAPTER TWELVE

— 1941 —

FEBRUARY

TUESDAY 11

Just as we were listening to the news old Mr Stewart appeared again with his collection of wolf-photographs. He must certainly have a gift for winning the confidence of animals; the secret of course being affectionate understanding and patience and it would almost appear that he has a more considerate love for animals than for human beings. About 7.0 while he still bent over me . . . we had word of Aunt Meg's death. When I shouted to S. that my father's sister had just died, he said: 'Ah! at rest from trouble,' and continued his elegy to the memory of a collie-bitch.

JULY

SATURDAY 5

Bill Montgomerie along bringing a friend George Bruce[1] to see me. Bruce a very likeable chap of 35 or so—writes verse. Is a nephew to F. G. Scott—but is not in awe of his 'Uncle Francis'. Montgomerie had been on a botany expedition and produced from his vasculum a few sprays bearing the one and only 'sma' white rose of Scotland',[2] the first time I could say with certainty I had looked on the national emblem.

SEPTEMBER

MONDAY 8

DICHT! AND DINNA BE DAMNED
(*Impromptu on the G string*)

Jim Finnel[3] ca's me Pilate*
(And maybe he's no far wrang),
F. G. Scott taks my bairns by the throat
And strangles maist o' their sang.

There's douceness in a douncome:
And sin friends wud wark ye weel,
I tak the lot frae Finnel and Scott—
And hae guid hope to grow hale.

Sae lat the hert be canty
Whether it flochter or fa';
And at ilka claut come up wi' a stot
Mair bouncy nor a ba'.

(*In his letter to-day J. F. proclaimed that I had washed
my hands, like Pilate, over the truth that confronted me in
the Pict Party Programme: Scott's analysis of my verse has
a great deal of truth in it.[4])

DECEMBER

THURSDAY 11

A further communication from Williams and Norgate to-day
in which they propose to issue *The Signature of Silence* in
brochure form if 300 sales can be assured. Again we meet the
conflicting values—the gesture of faith and the economic
limitations; the impasse between quality and quantity which
is the doom of our age. Here is a MS., according to their
reader's report, in which there are poems better than the
best of Housman, poems that transform the war-revulsion
of Sassoon into revelation, poems of Blakean vision, etc.,
etc.—in short, a book most needful to our time of conflict. And here are the monetary qualifications—curtailing

expenditure to £27 plus a guarantee; for after all there is no certainty that a most needful thing will be recognised by the needy. We have knocked at publishers' houses for nearly 20 years, and still await more than the half-open door; we'll continue to knock.

CHAPTER THIRTEEN

— 1942 —

JANUARY

MONDAY 12

Why is it that Amiel, with his literary gifts, is remembered not as poet or essayist but as a diarist? Surely from the fact that it was in his journal that he found a purpose; it became his need and his service to life—hence the absorption in which he could lose himself even when self-analysis was its theme. Here he gave himself away; and since the love of his task was constrained by need—he wrote with integrity; he saw himself through the eyes of imagination. Divided in his response to ordinary living he was in his confessions whole; here out of his weaknesses he was made strong. Such a sublimation of action is impossible to-day, for the individual is too deeply implicated in the social travail; the private embarrassments of the craftsman cannot be viewed in isolation from the problems of the community; and as that community is a frustrated thing manifesting divergent and partisan allegiances, there is a cleavage in the mind between the claims of art and society. This explains the lack of a major art in our time and why a preoccupation such as Amiel's would be now an evasion.

FRIDAY 30

A local character: My father called in at the office of Peter Brown (Pete Broon), the plasterer, yesterday and noticed a bust of Jesus in a corner; which Pete informed him he had begged from old Willie Mackay of the same craft. 'He had a hale cleckin o' plaister-casts; and whan he gied up his business he said: "Break up the lot o' them"; but I got that ane aff him: and *that* is my religion.' Pete left this last remark in its mystery to recount an incident from *Outward Bound* in which an elderly man when dying asks a companion to straighten a picture which isn't there. The friend to humour the old man made a few imaginary adjustments. 'I'll aye mind that,' continued Pete; 'for a week or twa eftir when my ain faither was deein he said to me: "Peter, that strap alang the wa' there isnae strecht." So I gaed owre and gien the place twa-three chaps wi' my knuckles, "Hoo's that noo?" I said: and the auld man nodded his heid and lookit contented like.'

SATURDAY 31

Yesterday's entry illustrates how anecdotes become confused in the retelling. When Alex Galloway called last night I mentioned the Pete Brown incident and asked Alex if he remembered the old man's anxiety about the badly-hung picture in *Outward Bound*. Alex was certain that there was no such occasion—but revealed that in *Lady Hamilton*, a film which has been on show for the week here, there is a scene like this. On questioning my father again, I learned that Pete *had* said something about *Lady Hamilton*; and it must have been then that he recalled his father's hallucination which, of course, happened some years ago. The 'coincidence' was therefore in the film—and, naturally, must have come home forcibly to Pete. It appears that Pete is a most rambling talker—and what with his confessions of stookie-faith, 'ghost' ships and moribund illusions, it is not surprising that Pops had become somewhat wandered in the sequences of association.

FEBRUARY

SATURDAY 21

THE PROPOSAL[1]
(A Whigmaleerie)

Rab Kelty was a widow-man;
But that was nocht byor'nar,
Sin three guid-wives were doun at Dron
A' kistit in ae corner.

As comfort for the hindmaist ane
He courtit Minnie Summers;
And ae day brocht her to the stane
That was abüne his kimmers.

Rab look't a whilie at the lair,
Syne wi' a sech said: 'Hinny,
Hoo wud ye like to be happit here?'
'I wudna mind,' said Minnie.

APRIL

FRIDAY 10

FOR ONIE BARDIE IN A BY-NEUK

Hae the folk a' passed ye by:
Are ye edg'd clean oot o' the thrang:
Has this man's cry and that man's cry
Rowted abüne your sang?

Hae ye chappit frae door to door
In hope o' the howff o' fame
And naebody has hecht ye owre;
And maist were awa frae hame?

Nae doot ye will ramp a while,
And glunsch on your luckless ware;
But or lang—gin the makin's leal—
You'll fash yoursel' nae mair.

But haud richt on your ain gait,
And ken, what I needna tell,
That aye through fame's hindmaist yett
The wark maun gang itsel'.

SATURDAY 18

ON
COMING UPON SOME VERSES
WHICH I COULD NOT RECALL HAVING WRITTEN

Queer it was to confront ye
And frae your ainsel' learn
That I nae langer kent ye
Wha aince had been my bairn.

And yet this canna shame me,
Or mak me mair alane,
Sin a' I'll hae to name me
Are bairns nae langer mine.

MONDAY 20

APRIL 1942

The light shines on our wrong
At the sun's ascending hour
When in the time of flower
These who must die are young.

These who must die are young;
And on their brows no bay:
Only the April day
For garland and for song.

MAY

SATURDAY 2

MORE CONFESSIONS FRAE CALEDONIA

Montgomerie, Scott and Grieve
Are no sae blate to blaw:
And yet I cud weel believe
I am prouder nor them a'.

For pride is a slicky carl
Wha aften, gin truth wud tell,
Walks doucely through the warl'
To keep himsel' to himsel'.

O! I doubt the thistle's my kin
For better or for waur,
And I hae yon look in my e'en
That cries: 'Bide a bit attowre!'

THURSDAY 19

A PICKLE STANE AND STOUR

There wudna be sae muckle girnin
And no sae muckle care
Gin folk wud mind the world was turnin
Lang, lang, or folk were here:

Gin folk wud mind that stars were luntin,
And through the pit-mirk birl'd,
Lang, lang, afore oor sün was glintin
Abüne a growthy warld.

Yet I maun awn a thocht maist human,
And monie folk wud share,
That there will aye be men and women
Girnin and fou o' care:

And that oor peerie-weerie stishie
On a pickle stane and stour
Can gar the hale o' the heavens hishie—
And God himsel' keek owre.

MONDAY 25

CADGER JIMMY[2]
(A Whigmaleerie)

Doun in the boddom o' his cartie
On the road to Tibbermuir
Cadger Jimmy's fou and herty
Roarin hame frae the fair.

My faither's dead, my mither's dottle,
My tittie's cowpit the creel;
My only brither is the bottle
And I've aye lo'ed him weel.

A canny beast is Jimmy's cuddie,
Saw Jimmy needna care
Roarin hame alang the roadie
Frae Perth to Tibbermuir.

My faither's dead, my mither's dottle,
Etc.

JUNE

TUESDAY 23

Finished reading A. C. Bradley's *Shakespearean Tragedy*
which has lain unread for 20 years: a work of profound penetration. Not only has it taught me much about Shakespeare;
but its analysis of those values which underlie Shakespeare's
tragic conception has in some measure confirmed my own

convictions embodied in *But the Earth Abideth*. I have
assumed that our age is one which by its debility of spirit
and the accumulated conditioning of events has proved
incapable of imaginatively experiencing the tragic aspect of
life; and that this failure necessitates the enduring of tragedy
by the flesh. What I have attempted to reveal in a very small
way in my poem-sequence is this relationship; and that the
conditions under which our generation suffers are those of
tragic fulfilment. As in tragic drama—the psychological
conflict; the reciprocity of action and consequence by which
at last the aggregation of misdeeds becomes a destructive
doom; the governance of a moral power over man to which
in freedom or in frustration he is ultimately obedient—all
these factors are manifest in our contemporary tribulation.
The pity, the mystery, the grandeur, the terror and the
reconciliation are also here—the guilt and the greatness of
man under the shining of eternity.

SUNDAY 28

CRUSTS O' KINDNESS

Whaur the Highgate ends at the water-side
You'll see an auld man stand:
The sea-maws are whitterin round his head
And snip the bread frae his hand.

Fair day or weet you will find him there
At the sel'same hour and place;
The white wings flichterin out o' the air,
And a fain look on his face.

And the thocht comes hame as you watch him stand
Sae raggity, auld and fail,
That the crusts o' kindness he hauds in his hand
Are a' he has kent himsel'.

SEPTEMBER

WEDNESDAY 9

Read a little book of verse entitled *Cage Without Grievance*,
by a 'modern Scot', W. S. Graham. Montgomerie's gift;
and inscribed on it by him is Marston's line: 'I feare

God onely know what Poets meane'—certainly applies to
Graham's stuff.

WEDNESDAY 23
Finished reading Amiel's *Journal Intime* to-day. How easy
for a critic to lapse into a patronising attitude towards this
most sensitive man who was so critical of himself. But
it is Amiel who reveals the world's malformities in the
undistorted mirror of his self-revelation; the harshness of
everyday humanity in the tender light of his compassion.
He was in truth a martyr to the ideal; and in remaining
faithful to his vision endured that sorrow which rests as a
vicarious burden upon the lovingkindness of the great. Thus
by the integrity of his self-judgment we are judged; and by
his communing made conscious of the world's communal
neediness which is the major cause of international discord
and strife. Before this rare soul's humility we are humbled,
and by the courage of his self-exposure we are challenged
to strip away our own dissimulations. Only the superficial
listener will apprehend no more than the confessions of a
hypochondriac spirit; but he who listens with his heart will
hear the exhortations of a prophet.

NOVEMBER

WEDNESDAY 4

SIC A HOAST

Sic a hoast hae I got:
Sic a hoast hae I got:
I dout my days are on the trot;
Sic a hoast hae I got.

Whauzlin like an auld tup,
I grup whatever's there to grup
And clocher half my stummick up;
Sic a hoast hae I got.

Physic, poultices and pills,
Reekin rousers, reemin yills,
Nane can shift this hell o' ills;
Sic a hoast hae I got.

> The delver at his deathly trade
> Gies a rattle wi' his spade;
> Blinks an e'e, and shaks his head;
> Sic a hoast hae I got.
>
> Sic a hoast hae I got:
> Sic a hoast hae I got:
> I dout my days are on the trot;
> Sic a hoast hae I got.

FRIDAY 6

Writing in the forenoon: Dinner: writing and reading in the afternoon. Have been troubled by a deep-seated cough which would not lift. Tea: After tea felt really out of sorts—the jokiness of the verses on the 4th having now given place to earnest. Got a hot drink and dosed with aspirin—which soon had me most beetrooty in complexion. Glad to get settled down for the night.

THURSDAY 12

If not any worse this morning—certainly not improved: Pops asked D. B. to look across: enjoyed my chicken soup: dozy in the afternoon: D. B. came in about 5.30: as I expected he found a patch of pneumonia at the base of the left lung: there is also a touch of pleurisy: as usual a formidable therapeutic list made up—one indeed begins to feel he is facing a dangerous foe when so many weapons of defence are mustered (a pun?) on the thoracic front.

FRIDAY 20

D. B. still wants me to have complete quiet for another week: must have been worse than I fancied.

MONDAY 23

Chest appears to be practically cleared now though I am bothered with an irritating cough and have very little pep—even when reading my eyes begin to tire in half an hour: must have got properly run down somehow—certainly hadn't been eating much for a while.

TUESDAY 24

Endeavoured to get some verses on to paper but there was no flow. . . . Our milkman Mr Dow (aged 36) died

of pneumonia to-day: had been too long, I doubt, in
lying up.

DECEMBER

WEDNESDAY 9

> Dull is the day but my wits are duller;
> And I mak nither sang, nor sonnet, nor siller.

TUESDAY 15
Began smoking again after a lapse of more than five
weeks—hadn't much pleasure from the few cigarettes I
savoured: staleness seems to have permeated most things.
I begin to realise that I must have been 'sickening' for a
fairly lengthy spell before I actually sickened: the poorish
quality of the majority of the verses written in the past three
or four months would suggest this.

CHAPTER FOURTEEN

— 1943 —

JANUARY

SATURDAY 2

Above the achievements of genius whether in the arts, leadership or construction, is there not a greatness that may be shared by the most ordinary human being; a greatness in which so many men of genius have been deficient? And is not this common greatness, which is yet the highest, a magnanimity in the acts and the relationships of everyday; a faithfulness to the commonplace which demands a humankindness and self-forgetting more spontaneous than in the purposiveness of art or leadership. Thus we may claim that under this defining of greatness the greatest men and women are unrecognised and unknown.

SATURDAY 16

Had the notion to note down the contents of my pockets:

Breast-pocket:—Coloured handkerchief and small round mirror.

Left side-pocket:—Coloured handkerchief.

Right side-pocket:—White handkerchief: blue tam-o'-shanter which I wear when having my pillows changed: an oblong piece of rubber: small round rubber: styptic pencil in wooden holder: small penknife: two pencil stubs: six collar-supports: two bone buttons: four paper-fasteners: two very small safety-pins: six match ends which I use as tooth-picks: four farthings and one Indian quarter-anna: also little 'mascot' Scotch-terrier.

TUESDAY 26

If we agree that between the origin of Christianity and the Renaissance we witness the rise and decline of community as the focal centre of human consciousness, and if we agree that between the Renaissance and our own time we witness the rise and decline of individuality as another such centre, then may we not assume that we are now entering a period wherein men will be faced by the challenge to evolve a way of life in which by creative co-operation the communal and individual needs and responsibilities are balanced. As the basis for such a unity the whole earth must be acknowledged as our allegiance, and that nationality can no longer be a sovereignty. Material need is already compelling men towards this realisation, and it is probably inevitable that at the moment materialistic concepts are predominant: but the operation of religious faith must follow if human schemes are to satisfy not only the social but the solitary aspirations of man as person.

MARCH

SATURDAY 13

Morgan the banker and Benet the poet died yesterday: B.B.C. had much to say of the former but little of the latter.

MEMORIAL

Having for rule the steady standard—gold,
The worth of banker Morgan soon is told:
But only time holds in his hand the measure
Which can compute the sum of Benet's treasure.

PASSPORT TO PARADISE

Morgan and Benet being dead
Up to the gates of heaven sped,
And each upon his journey took
For passport into bliss—a book.

A janitor with careful mien
Peered at the tokens handed in;
Then with an archangelic frown
He set the banker Morgan's down.

'Sir! in your passport there appears
Such stains as Benet's—blood and tears;
And yet I turn your bank-book down
Since these mute words are not your own.'

MONDAY 15

If one may judge from the young men and women in their
twenties who call here—one must accept that exceptionally
few of them have any interest in serious or solid reading;
indeed many seem to read hardly anything at all. Last night,
for example Margaret Boyce admitted that she had never
read a book through; and her boy friend Jack Riley claimed
that once as a test of will-power he *forced* himself to read
through three books by Conrad. It would certainly appear
that the inter-war years had produced a generation restless,
and recreated by light amusements. The cinema has become
their literature, art and music; and in consequence they have
little desire to give that additional concentration necessary
in sharing the masterpieces of the arts and of the theatre:
by circumstance and by inclination they are satisfied with
the second-hand; modern dances and modern dance music
are symptomatic of this easy satisfaction.

MAY

WEDNESDAY 12

Historic date—definitely stopped smoking—not a moral
victory, merely the result of the gradual lessening of the
pleasure I had from puffing a cigarette: at last the pleasure
has become nil.

FARE-THEE-WELL

For many years Tobac and I
Have been to each a faithful friend;
And now, without a single sigh,
Our comradeship is at an end.

With pleasure, which at last departs,
Affection too is fugitive;
And this is true for human hearts—
Where no joy is love cannot live.

Douglas Young steppit in looking quite fit after his jailing:[1]
jawed on all the afternoon.

JUNE

SUNDAY 20
Re-read MacDiarmid's *Scots Unbound*—some fine lyrics;
but the 'thocht' in the lengthy poems confounds the poetry;
why must Grieve so often use his verse as a shopwindow
for displaying curiosities of erudition? But I could do with
some of his energy at the moment—no verve.

WEDNESDAY 23
Early in the afternoon Douglas Young stalked in: monologue for the rest of the afternoon which suited me—
Douglas though something of a conversational conveyer-belt
isn't a bore.

JULY

SUNDAY 4

EPITAPH
(A Whigmaleerie)

They delv'd a saft hole
For Johnnie McNeel:
He aye had been droll
But folk likit him weel.

The bell gied a toll;
And Mess John in his goun
Spak guid-words for the soul
As Johnnie gaed doun.

On a wee, mossy-knoll,
That's green a' the year,
A stane-letter'd scroll
Tells Johnnie liggs there.

Nae lang rigmarole;
Juist—*Johnnie McNeel*
Was aye a bit droll
But folk likit him weel.

D. B. Low looked in at 11.30. He thought me even thinner than on his last visit. After a sounding he said there was a cavity at the apex of my right lung—I take this as a death sentence. Actually I believe my left lung is in a worse condition.[2]

MONDAY 5

From now on these pages will as a rule contain only the reports of factual doings—with comment here and there if such suggests itself. Occasionally a poem may appear amongst the prose—but for a time now the creative verve has been weakening with the weakening body.

† Yesterday at 11.30, while I was yet dressing after my Sabbath ablutions, D. B. Low came in to sound my chest—now a corrugated wheeze-box. After roaming all regions he came back to a spot at the top of my right lung. It must have been a slightly ludicrous scene as I lay with my shirt collarless and my head encased in a blue beret set at an acute angle while David invited me to whisper one, one, one, one. The whispering definitely certified a cavity—and I suppose David realised, as surely as myself, that he was listening-in to a grave. I had a fleeting impulse to ask: 'How long do you think I may live?' But refrained as I considered it was rather premature, and also because I was not quite certain that I wished to know just yet.

† And why the beret? While washing myself *in toto* on Sundays, or at times when my pillows are being changed etc: I wear the beret to keep my hair in about—and also to hide the fact that the front of my dome has now a Shakespearean bareness.

† I do not know what D. B. said to the folks—but I am sure they have guessed that my lungs aren't too good.

TUESDAY 6

† For a month or two I have assumed in a casual way that I hadn't very long to live; and already I have some knowledge

† Entries so indicated are from *The Diary of a Dying Man*.

of one's reactions to a fatal certainty. I thought 'Now that a major fact has confronted you the minor happenings of everyday will take on their true proportions: you will cease to react with violent outbursts of irritated speech or gesture when little frustrations annoy; the presence of the major fact will remind you how small and transient are these vexations.' But as yet I have grown towards this serene stature only a very little way; though I seem to sense a gradual awareness of a still centre within myself.

† There is an increase in day-dream, in which I find I am often making elaborate preparation for the disposal of my cadaver and my manuscripts. Probably it is a compensation—but, since I have begun to accept that death is not so far away, I have also accepted as surety that I shall be remembered as a poet. How strange the fancies of semi-wakefulness; the other morning I thought: 'My right nostril is Scottish but my left is English.'

WEDNESDAY 7
† The suffering of a million casualties in accumulation is yet the suffering of one man; the ultimate death-struggle the striving of one. In dying, therefore, we consider our own disintegration as worthy of contemplation as any other. But what of the multitudinous bereaved: the innumerable repercussions from grief? How many faces that are sorrowful that might now be glad?

† I was amused the other day by a story reported to have had a local origin. A Perth tailor named Rattray, who has or had a shop in Princes Street, was the originator. When a small boy he had been given a kippered herring for his tea; and, after he had removed as much of the flesh as he could from bones and skin, found a large accumulation of odd bits on his plate. When he had considered this for a while he remarked to his parents: 'Jesus must hae gien kippers to the multitude, for I've far mair left owre than I had at the start.'

† Just before tea I read the ballad, 'Edward'; of its kind it is as great a poem as 'The Wife of Usher's Well': there is the imprint of a fine artist upon this ballad as the form of the verses in itself reveals.

† For two or three months now my sight hasn't been just so clear. Might the tension of the focusing muscles have been slightly affected by the more sunken eyes?

FRIDAY 9

† To know that one is nearing the end of his life becomes a revelation of how dilatory one has been in the years when death seemed far away. My own days have been but loosely filled with accomplished tasks; in comfort and quiet the tempo of one's living tends to become more and more easy-moving; the fulfilling of one's busyness more and more liable to be prolonged by the thought—'There is always to-morrow.' So much that I ought to have completed remains fragmentary or wholly unexpressed; but one must be on guard against the suggestion that environment was a major factor: laziness isn't a topographical outcrop.

† Mrs Vass in the kindness of her ample bosom brought me a bottle of concentrated orange-juice to pep up the vitamins. I find on the label that the quantity suitable for me is that for an expectant mother. Well, I suppose I may claim to be both father and mother of such bairns as I produce; and certainly I am ever expectant that they have the breath of life in them.

SATURDAY 10

† D. B. looked in to let me know the report on the sample of sputum which he asked for lately—the finding was positive, of course: yet to have this unquestionable proof brought the certainty of death into clear focus: there is now no longer any scope for fanciful hopes. When D. B. was sounding me I asked if he'd any idea how long I might last. Why do the doomed always ask this question: probably in order to complete what may be completed within the period: yet is it not a useless query since the doom though certain is nevertheless centred in uncertainty; D. B. could not say which was the proper answer. When the folks came into my room, after David had completed his listening, he began to suggest how I might have more fresh air and sunshine. My window could be made to open in the lower half of it which consists of a large pane of plate glass, very heavy and

fixed into its frame: three much smaller panes open on the top-half of the window and let in more than enough air for my liking. Then I might be transferred (how?) on sunny days to the summer-house which is almost entirely all glass, and on any day of even moderate sunshine a place to swelter in. I listened for a little while then said, 'O! I haven't time for all these capers.' This sent David into laughter—and he accepted the retort as a final negative on his proposals.

SUNDAY 11

† When I looked out on the garden this morning and saw the 'blue bells' I said to myself spontaneously, 'I wonder if I'll see these next year?' This is the first time the thought has presented itself: the awareness of the certainty has gone deeper.

† There are dangers, of course, in writing a diary such as this, and unless one's attitude remained detached, contemplating the self as a subject (or if you prefer it object) under a mind willing to understand all the phenomena of somatic change and psychological reaction, yet implicated only as a sympathetic observer unbiassed by sentimentality and self-regard. This is the ideal and beyond complete adoption; but if the recorder of a diary such as this is vigilant in checking any pitiful self-indulgence he will approximate fairly near to the detached observer. Otherwise what should be a chronicle of common humanity will become increasingly the exposure of a self-centering individual: a process of dying inward instead of a dissipation into the vastness of day and the movement of human concerns and expectancies.

At half past one Tom Scott strode in, having come home from West Africa: very little change in him after his two years in the tropics. Brought some poems for me to look over with a critical eye. Much experimentation in his verse in English; his solitary poem in Scots, and his first, exhibited the chief fault of all the younger school: many of the words haven't passed through the blood and the imagination; they remain counters and are often set into the wrong context. The young school, Smith,[3] Young, Scott, etc., probably take their efforts over-seriously: more detachment would imply more humour—and humour is an excellent judge of poetic fitness and misproportion.

MONDAY 12

Mrs Rolley looked in with her son Allan, a very tall pilot-officer at 20 or so. A most pleasant lad with an alert manner. As we sympathised with his mother, whose home is on the English south coast where the siren wails almost daily and nightly, I noticed a quiet smile on Allan's face. What did it mean? There was nothing superior or cruel in it: it seemed rather the smile of one who belonged to a different world and to whom the anxious scuttling of civilians had something ludicrous about it: to the mind that was smiling this scrambling world remained far away so that the suffering and the destruction were but remote gestures and outcries too faint to leave their impress on compassion.

† We are strange creatures who can find cause for exhilaration even in disaster. As I lifted this diary yesterday I was sensible of such a reaction to misfortune: is it not a distinctive state of living to be under a doom and yet with time enough to contemplate the implications of such a state? Few are privileged by environment and temperament to explore without hastening the last reaches of the journey which ends in silence; to note, with what fidelity is ours, the thoughts and emotions which are dulled or stimulated by the close companionship of death; to sense in some measure the mystery of life and death in their mutuality so that in approaching the final halt we no longer ask who is our guide.

† When my top-sheet was brought in from the sun the other day I wondered for a little while what its fresh smell reminded me of—and then I recognised that it was a dairy; and particularly a Miss MacGregor's dairy in Hospital Street where first I inhaled the rich, creamy smell. There I used to get my Grannie's milk when a very small boy; and I often played outside the door.

TUESDAY 13

Writing in the forenoon: one keeps on adding words to words and does not question if any reader will turn a discriminating eye upon them: the attitude in no way differs from a craftsman and his craft. This is the job to be done; and it would be all the further from excellence if the craftsman, as he wrought, saw in his task a possible memorial to his ability. The absorption is the job; and serenity of spirit is found in the knowledge that nothing of true value can fall out of the fabric of reality: the utilitarian, mechanic and imitative making supplies the transitory need and crumbles away; the truly creative becomes a part of the structure of life.

† I finished reading a *Book of Scottish Verse* yesterday—edited by George Burnett. What a number of minor Scottish poets there are of the latter part of last century and the beginning of this who are remembered in one or two poems. How circumscribed the themes; how limited the vocabulary; yet within their narrow field they were assured of the usage of their speech: if their poetry had little range or depth, it spoke confidently of what had been experienced: how different from the work of the young Modern Scots who employ many words but few have a root.

WEDNESDAY 14

† In his misfortune, even in the onset of death, man discovers consolations and compensations: he will not admit that any condition can be wholly disastrous or any loss complete. And this is but another aspect of his faithfulness to life; his refusal to believe that life could ever be confounded and come under total eclipse; that goodness could pass away utterly under the accumulated forces of evil. *A propos* this attitude I too begin to discover minor conditions which alter for the better now that they are modified by the limitations of time. I have had excellent teeth; and even after fourteen years without dental attention they remain very good though a few require stopping. For eleven years I have had an abscess at the root of the first incisor on the right side of my upper jaw. I have been lucky in that it usually drains away to the outside; now and then it becomes troublesome when the outlet gets sealed for a while. However at some date I'd have to get the tooth removed and the others attended to—now

for compensation I have the knowledge that I shall dodge
this bit of bother. And so with my eyes which have also
served me well, but not so well lately; I shan't require to
use glasses set at some peculiar angle due to my 'low-down'
position. Strangely insignificant fragments of satisfaction set
against the enormity of life and death.

THURSDAY 15
† I have something of the Swiftean disgust at unpleasant smells; and when Mrs Stirling came in stinking
of cheap scent and disinfectant I involuntarily said in
thought:—'Thank God! I sleep by myself.' During the
intensity of passion the odours of the excited flesh though
sensed are ignored: but, with this necessitous exception,
who would not prefer a solitary bed?

FRIDAY 16
† With death in the breast it is necessary for the body to
conserve its remaining strength; it draws into itself avoiding
unnecessary contacts and expenditure of energy: its duty is
now to sustain as long as possible the contemplative mind
that it may gather-in the last gleanings of experience which,
in their turn, sustain the imagination. The body must come
home to itself, but still it is the sanity of the spirit to go forth
forgetting the doom that is upon its flesh and the lassitude
that at last will silence all communication.
   † It is this conservation of the fated flesh which explains
why in the passed three months I have ceased to think about
women, or indulge in amorous imaginings. This abstinence
has not been aided by any moral resolutions which the
nearness of the grave might have called up: the only exercise
of will power has been to cut short any day-dream tending
towards sensuality, and this ascetic gesture has been made
but very rarely. How many reformers who condemn the
licentiousness of others may be unconscious hypocrites,
having never known desire in its full potency.

SATURDAY 17
† To experience in a state of fatality a certain relish is not
only a sanifying response but also a warning lest we are
accepting death too complacently. All of us have known a

mood in which we would lay down the burden of mortality
and sleep in a forgetfulness from which there is no waking:
but the mood has passed, and the cowardice of it which had
valued one's comfort above the gift of life. Now that I have
received the guarantee that at some hour not so very far
away the restlessness of the flesh will be silenced and sleep
assured, I must face the query whether I bid farewell to life
with full consciousness of the gift which is being returned,
or whether I take the hand of death too readily. I have no
family responsibilities; I believe that my poetry has begun
to show signs that I have written down all I had to say; I
have the conviction that certain of these words will become
a part of the literature of our time. These factors all tend
towards a fairly easy acceptance of death. But there are
others. In a few years I would be left alone: I might in time
become the inmate of a hospital: an extension of the arthritis
might render me a complete invalid unable to move a limb.
Confronted by these possibilities an element of cowardly
satisfaction is in the calm acknowledgment of doom. We
shrink from certain conditions of living and thereby would
set conditions upon our acceptance of life.

SUNDAY 18
As Sunday's clean-up is a fully stripped affair I can see
the cadaver in the buff. I was somewhat shocked myself,
yesterday (that's this date, of course), to note how much
flesh I had lost. I trust this drastic period of slimming is
over for the time, otherwise like the old soldiers I might
fade away before I had completed the odd jobs which I'd
like to see finished. The most important of these is 'From
a Note-book', a selection of revised entries in my diary,
my collection of English lyrics now to be entitled, 'The
Expectant Silence',4 and my collection of Scots poems on
my own burgh—under the title, 'Yon Toun'.

  † Just as it is impossible for me to understand anyone
who considers G. B. Shaw to be as fine a dramatist as
Shakespeare, so I think it most strange that anyone should
consider that claret is as fine a wine as port. The warmth,
colourfulness, rich flavour, pungency without harshness
and full-bodiedness of port are qualities which one might

transfer to the work of Shakespeare. In comparison claret is cool, subdued in colour, somewhat insipid in flavour, smooth and uniform in drinking without the unexpectancy of tang and taste which is found as port goes over the throat. In drinking claret one does not feel any stirring of abandonment; rather is one conscious of a medicinal element and that one imbibes for one's 'good'. So the plays of Shaw are for one's 'good'; cool, uninflamed and smooth-moving dramas of instruction; in short, claret has the excellences of prose and port the excellences of poetry.

MONDAY 19

† I recall but rarely that I am under the shadow of death, and this is natural behaviour for the day is full of the abundance of little duties and distractions, and the bright presence of life turns our attention to the movement and interrelationship of the ordinary sights and sounds which pass across the small orbit of our tangible world. Situated as I am, still almost at ease, only the perversity of a morbid spirit could withhold a normal response in contact with earth and one's fellows: and while strength is yet sufficient there will remain an alertness ready to recognise a transitory manifestation of beauty, and to find emblems of everlastingness in familiar meetings. And when debility brings a dullness over the sense and the self-hood draws back further and further from the shining day, even in the increasing darkness remembrance may still remain to assure that each day dawns in praise and departs in expectancy.

TUESDAY 20

† How trifling as yet the inconveniences which trouble me. A prolonged spell of coughing to dislodge an obstruction only four or five times a day; the waking in a night-sweat (not excessive) three or four times; the breathlessness and palpitation after exertion; and a few racked muscles. These indications of illness do not disturb and rarely remind me of catastrophe: it is the look of my face that sometimes makes me wonder if I may have time to complete what I have planned: though I eat quite well, and the most sustaining fare, the hollows in the cheeks and at the temples remain the same. Before settling for sleep I draw the sheet high up

each side of my head to cover the ears and I am reminded unmorbidly of John Donne in his shroud.

WEDNESDAY 21
† During my talk with Peter Hepburn yesterday he recalled a temporary English teacher we had after the beginning of the last war. McKinlay was his name though neither of us could recollect it yesterday. He was a smallish, abstracted man with a little military moustache and boots which appeared too large for him. His tie very often revealed that he had been breakfasting on egg and dining on soup; and, no doubt, reading as he fed. After the last period, one would sometimes discover him at the pavement edge contemplating his large boots half of which stuck over the kerb. Occasionally he was referred to as 'Charlie Chaplin' but the nickname never took hold: perhaps he seemed too serious for it was rarely that we saw him smile. He could not be called a capable teacher for his control was lax and few paid any attention to his words. Somehow I sensed his keen appreciation of literature and my own interest was quickened and increased so that I date my joy in great writing from the teaching of McKinlay. He may have been our English teacher for a session—certainly no more—before joining the army. Rumours came through of McKinlay in the backward squad as he proved so muddled at drill; but these may have originated from the oversized boots. If backward, he had not been so very long, for at no wide interval from his departure we found his obituary notice in the school-magazine. There we learned that he had written poetry, and among the quotations was a memorable line, 'As gulls that follow the mast-light'. I suppose he would be no more than 27 years old.

THURSDAY 22
† Death which is so momentous an event in its relationship to the individual is a fact I seem to have accepted long ago and asked no questions. My attitude is not indifference but detachment, and this may have come from my practice of poetry which demands a stepping out of the circle of one's private interests and prejudices. And this aspect of generality is also found in my love which has never been

centred deeply in any individual but has responded to the commonalty of earth and mankind. So death has remained for me freed from dogmas and nearest implications of relationship; and because of this I have felt no urge to peer beyond the grave. I can assert from my own experience and expectation no particular certainties concerning the personality of God and the nature of an after-life; holding for faith that the righteousness of life is incorruptible and that all eventuality is under the rule of creative law. Such a bare belief is based upon stoicism rather than the love of one's kind; it is pagan rather than christian; it is obedient to the demands of art rather than of life: but as yet it is my credence.

If at the end of our life—even if it end early—we have not attained balance and content, it is not lack of days or the circumscription of our environment that is to be blamed, but our own deficiency in sympathetic insight and in co-operation. When the fullness of life is comprehended then the nothingness of the self is revealed: then we are ready to admit that all is gifted to be made use of and returned; and that blame is within our self.

FRIDAY 23
† Once or twice lately the thought has gone over my mind that the end of the day and sleep were not so far off: this thought in its moment was pleasant. The weariness which prompted the thought was produced byy a few factors: a certain amount of muscular strain comes from coughing; tiredness of the eyes is not uncommon; but above all irritations is the general bodily discomfort caused by the lack of flesh on my bones. Every little while I am made aware of a painful pressure, and seek to shift my bones into a more comfortable position but soon slide back into a disturbing one. Fortunately by a regular application of methylated spirit and talcum powder, my skin though chafed in places has not broken: I have been lucky enough never to have had a bed-sore. Yet the fact that these little strains and discomforts should have prompted the thought of unconsciousness, with an accompanying feeling of satisfaction, reveals how far my cadaver has lost its resiliency.

SATURDAY 24

† One thought which recurs again and again is whether
the folks would complete their years in greater content
and serenity, or whether their last years would close in
greater sadness and disappointment if I died before them.
To predecease them would certainly cause grief, perhaps
be the ending of a hope that I might grow into a poet of
international reputation, would take away a preoccupation
for which there could be no substitute—hence, in mother
at least, the danger of brooding and of enlarging loss; and
would end many contacts with youngish minds, eccentrics,
and men and women of genuine depth of character. On
the other hand there would be an easement of physical
strain due to numerous services which are done for me
every day; they would escape the sense of frustration and
irritation when, if they were spared to very old age, their
tasks had to be performed by outsiders; and the ceasing
of that fretting thought which stirs the affection to anxious
speculation on what may happen to me when I am no longer
under their care.

SUNDAY 25

Now is the season when the war is most openly exposed
in contrast with natural living. Again the generosity of
life is revealed in the abundance of fruit and grain now
ripened to fullness: an abundance from which all may be
satisfied without struggle or craft. And added to the joy
of bodily sufficiency is the joy given to the mind which
looks upon the coloured beauty of autumn. Against this
world of beauty and beneficence the havoc of the striving
nations destroys the comeliness of common earth. Harvest
lands are blasted into fields of desolation, and where the
harvester had rejoiced is barren soil littered with twisted
metal and riven bodies. When faith in life degenerates then
death becomes our certainty.

† The spirit comes in its own chosen moment; yet the
spirit cannot act unless the flesh [is] alive in expectancy
and the blood flowing in urgency. About a worn body the
spirit must flutter vainly or gaining entrance can quicken
only broken utterances. A period of debility would therefore

instruct the creative mind to guard against bodily excesses
which in time coarsen not only the senses, so that they no
longer apprehend the finer manifestations of sensuousness,
but also the emotions that lose their capability of spontaneous response. This does not imply asceticism for the
richer our world of sense the more comprehensive our
world of the imagination. But there should be nothing
deliberate in our relationship to sensuous knowledge if it
is to become the wisdom of the flesh; as the acquirement
of spiritual wisdom it must be grown into, and become
as it were blended with the blood; a passing sensation
changed into a surviving experience, emotive in the heart
and conscious in the mind. The spirit is not elevated by the
despisal of the flesh, nor the body liberated by the spurning
of the spirit; only when honour is between them can truth
be revealed in figurements of beauty.

MONDAY 26
About 7.30, Jim Finlayson stepped in, and his entry after
so many years, and his welcome took place quite naturally,
as if he had been here last week. Not very much difference
in Jim.

† One sign of the physical enfeeblement which I have
known for a year or so is the desire for absolute rest
after a stretch of writing or reading; a stretch which
may be no more than half an hour. Not so long ago
I had no wish to doze-off for 10 minutes or so during
the day; but now I can pass into a half-sleep within a
very short space of time after shutting my eyes. Such an
ever-present tendency cannot but have its influence upon
the brain, so that the sluggishness of the blood produces
(at least in part) a corresponding sluggishness of thought.
Under a condition such as this, it is all the more necessary
to refrain from attempting to force the creative moment:
such moments will be rarer, and more tenuous, and easily
lost by any show of wilful interference. Resignation to the
inevitable and a waiting in quiet expectancy is the strength
of weakness. The moments of illumination and testimony
will be few but they will remain unflawed by debility and
anxiousness.

WEDNESDAY 28
Sometimes when I feel my temporal ridges which seem to
grow sharper every day I wonder if I am going to have
time to complete the various tasks which I should like to
see completed. Truly I can now fully appreciate Andrew
Marvell's lines –

> 'But at my back I always hear
> Time's wingéd chariot hurrying near.'

My main concern is 'From a Note-book' which will not
reach book-size before another six months or so. To know
that I would be unable to complete this collection would
indeed prove to be a frustration and a retribution since
the book might have been in print by now had I worked
persistently and not spasmodically upon it. One can but go
on now in expectancy.

FRIDAY 30
† The other day the thought came to me that I no longer
whistle and sing; but this is no indication of depression,
its cause is poor respiration: the singing often comes up
in the silence. However, we have here yet another proof
of how dependent is the spirit upon the expressiveness of
the flesh.

SATURDAY 31
† Whatever our own condition—how richly abundant is
every day in shapes and sounds of fulfilment and gaiety.
There are numberless guardians that stand between us and
despondency so long as the body is not overwrought by pain
and the mind by weariness; and so long as the environment
is not wholly destitute or shut in from communication with
cheerful beings and a glimpse of the natural world. Every
day there are in normal surroundings the green life of
earth and the spaciousness of the sky; there is song and
music ready to descend out of the clouds; and there is
the passing gayness of children, glimpsed perhaps as the
transiency of joy but no less real than the enduring grass
or the blue arch of the sky. This is the wonder of life
that in the midst of exuberance and merriment is death;
not as a terrifying phantom but as an ordinary man or

woman quieted into a listening silence which yet shares the indestructible abundance. Day after day the glory of life is made manifest; but life's gifts come not only into the hands of the strong; the weak also partake with the strong, and even the dying have their portion of a bounty which is denied to none.

AUGUST

SUNDAY I

It is very difficult to assess the poetry of De la Mare. Compared with Davies and Housman (for example) he is the most comprehensive poet of the three and has definitely created a world of the imagination; but Davies and Housman have a reality in their poems which is often absent from De la Mare and in the optimism of the one and the fatalism of the other we are ever conscious of listening to human utterance, the warmth of the flesh is in the words. De la Mare's world has regions that have never known the sun; where the atmosphere is so thin and moon-sodden that only bloodless and attenuated creatures could exist there: creatures half-human, half-phantom, that appear to be dissolving in the dream of the dreamer.

† Two or three times within the last month I have experienced unnormal sensations when in a very light drowsiness during the night. A few nights ago I had a congested feeling in the lower regions of the body, and as I tried by massage to ease the irritation, which was not painful to any marked degree, I had the sensation that the area of my belly had been considerably lessened and that I had my hands on a very small surface of skin so that I was greatly restricted in my attempts to ease the congestion. Last night I had a stranger experience. I fancy I had been asleep for a little while but awoke with a feeling of general discomfort and a patch or two of pain where my back and hips had been chafed—but not skinned. Again I had a sensation of congestedness but this time in the chest. Not wholly wakeful I began to mutter, and sometimes to say aloud, phrases of four words or so which might have

come from ballads. This continued for a while and was, no doubt, an attempt to gain some relief from my unease. All the phrases were uttered slowly as by a person who was worn out. I forget what I said with the exception of one phrase which intimated that 'It was owre late'. I suppose a body and mind condition such as the above is dependent upon a particular degree of discomfort and awareness: a little more pain or sensibility, and this state of consciousness would be eliminated.

MONDAY 2

Just as the common day is filled with fullness of life and has its strangeness, wonder, beauty and terror, so are ordinary folk rich in variety and act magnanimously and meanly, passionately and quietly, hopefully and in despair. But through all the folly and the foibles, the pettiness and the self-seeking, the superstition and the savagery, the true flame of life still gleams, and at the challenge of another's destitution, frailness or danger is ready to warm into generous action; so that from time to time we are astonished by the heroic greatness of the ordinary human spirit.

† So far I find few if any indications of that growth into serenity which I surmised would follow the confronting of premature death. Actually during the past week or two I have been cursing and swearing more and more due to an increase in bony irritation and the impossibility of coming upon a restful position that remains comparatively comfortable for more than half an hour. Sometimes I am shamed by the childish desire to roar in anger when a shift of position brings a torturous pressure on a spinal ridge. Even a night of hardly-broken sleep fails to refresh the body; tiredness still remains in the morning and drowsiness steals too many minutes from the waking day. But the cursing ought to come under better control lest from habit one begin to cry too readily at the touch of pain. The time will come when weakness may lessen the power to endure; then the body itself would seem to moan and murmur; and the tendency to such a subjugation of the will were increased by peevish outcries and curses while yet the mind was unclouded.

TUESDAY 3

† This afternoon the Rev W. Young from Glenfarg introduced himself as a lover of poetry including my own. He
has been retired for a good many years due to heart-trouble;
but I fancy that his cannie style is older than his ailment. If,
however, he displayed nothing of the visible signs of having
been an energetic parson, yet his naturalness, frankness
and kindliness may have done more good than numerous
meetings and up-to-the-minute sermons. He looked a man
of sixty-five. After a few remarks about my verse he
confessed that he had attempted to be a poet many times,
and that he would like to recite a few. Standing at the
foot of my bed he began his little recital speaking with an
intonation not much better than sing-song and in a slow
tempo which never varied. But the three sets of verses were
by no means ludicrous; and in a poem on the cuckoo he
had an image of some uniqueness, comparing the bird to
an idiot boy lost in the woods and crying out inarticulate
words. It is true 'we are all poets': some wholly mute,
some able to utter a few syllables, some capable singers
who yet remain no more than imitators, the genuine minor
poets ranging from the creator of a handful of lyrics to a
'little master', and then the few masters themselves who
have surmounted their individuality without discarding it,
and become the representatives of the age: men who, by an
inner compulsion, looked unwaveringly upon the good and
the evil.

WEDNESDAY 4

D. B. Low in about 4.30: sounded me and rediscovered the
cavity at the top of the right lung: I still feel that it is the
left lung that is more damaged. D. B. asked me to listen-in
to myself but I couldn't hear anything.

SUNDAY 8

† Many of my dreams now belong to that type in which one
is endeavouring to resolve something. All are most indefinite
and hazy in setting, and are accordingly rarely remembered.
Whatever the problem, and it may be as simple as arranging
lines of writing in correct order, the task is never completed;
but there is never a feeling of anxiety or anger at the

frustration—though I believe on some occasions there has been a sense of increasing tiredness. I cannot say for certain if one usually wakens from such a dream—certainly one does so sometimes. The origin of this sort of dream is, of course, bodily discomfort—and the effort upon effort to reach a solution is a parallel to the difficulty of finding a position in which one may rest. It is rather strange that the dream is free from anger—for I often get angry at the seeming impossibility of coming upon a comfortable position. Apart from the lack of liveliness there are one or two particular reasons for my forgetfulness as regards dreams. Now that circumstance has given a certain definiteness to the future, and now that I rarely think of women, there is a large elimination of tension and intensity both from day-dream and dream. Not only is there a curtailment of emotional 'subject-matter' for dreams to work upon with the consequence (which we may assume with assurance) that there will be fewer dreams, but the weakness of the accompanying emotion must leave only a faint impression on the mind.

TUESDAY 10
† How difficult, when invalidism is known to be progressive and finally fatal, to avoid an increasing consideration of the self. The therapeutic precautions in themselves are often limitations which others must share—hence they become concessions made to the individual. Already I begin to meet the temptation of self-pity by which one looks at himself against the background of the invalid state and not the normal day; with the implication that normality must be adapted to keep the abnormal in comparative comfort. So one might easily slide into complete ego-centricity relating all happenings not to general existence but to the particular corner of existence in which a life dwindled. This condition of a growing self-absorption is at this hour of time less excusable than in peace, when throughout half the world millions are in destitution, hunger and slavery, and millions are being mutilated or slaughtered. How easily a small inconvenience can cover the sun and make us forget the misery of a universe; and the tragic element in self-pity

is this, that at last the power of maintaining proportion between the world and the self is lo . and is not known to have been lost since what is now a world is within the deathly confines of a wholly involved self.

WEDNESDAY 11

† To-day drowsiness has been most persistent and many a time my eyes have shut, and I have become semi-conscious or entered an upper level of sleep. The total length of time used up in this way must have been considerable; and I fancy that the effect on the mind cannot be beneficial: indeed I am sensible now and then of mental dullness. It is true that last night I was more restless than usual and was awake many times; but there is no doubt that drowsiness is a condition which could rapidly increase in frequency; and in a while would be an irresistible habit. To reach such a state would, of course, be the end of any consistent work; and one would live almost an animal existence. My physical position is wholly conducive to the oncome of sleep, set at an obtuse angle which necessitates both head and body support: so I loll back among many pillows as one who invites a visitation from Morpheus. Had I been able to have sat up nearer the right-angle position, then the position would have been one of alertness as if one were arising; but as I am I sink back towards the grave-hole of oblivion.

THURSDAY 12

† The poet in his knowledge of life's glory is apt to disregard the unworthy qualities in human nature: his optimism often assumes that men are actually the magnanimous beings which they might be. Yet his error of judgment is on the right side, since daily there are the innumerous acts of self-forgetfulness which, in their accumulative human generosity, are the very bones which sustain the social body and the blood which animates it. Other poets in love with earth and natural beauty tend to concentrate on the darker aspects of human existence, and see man as a wayward creature disturbing by his unruliness the harmonious background of the seasons. Such poets are limited in vision and lack something of human kindness. Seen in true perspective against the world man assumes the

dignity of his heirship: when the loveliness and the grandeur of the earth dissolve in our moments of sorrow or suffering it is then that we turn to a human face and seek a meaning beyond the tangible.

FRIDAY 13

Why do we wish to be remembered even when none remain who looked upon our face? Surely, though it must retain an element of self-consideration, it is a last acknowledgment that we need to be loved; and having gone from all touch we trust that memory may, as it were, keep our unseen presence within the borders of day. But to be remembered were also a ratification of having given our fellows a gift of service, however small, which brought them bodily or mental satisfaction. Yet from this are we not taught that it is the deed that [is] primal in relationship. If the deed prove creative and comprehensive enough its influence is remembered though its author may become no more than a name and the civilisation in which he thrived be no more than a blurred chronicle.

TUESDAY 17

† When talking to Allan Morton yesterday reference was made to an Auchterarder man, Bain, who lost his life in a fight with some tinkers. As I like when possible to picture a man with some accuracy I asked Allan about his build. 'Man,' said Allan, 'he was just your height and build; aye, I'd say, exactly like yoursel'; he was a swank lad, richt enough.' This reference to 'a swank lad', I must confess, gave me a pleasant feeling: it was fine to know that I had looked such a lad.

WEDNESDAY 18

† PROSPECT

D. B. Low my medico
Pronounced with bed-side gravity:
'I fear, I fear, that I can hear
The echo of a cavity.'

Ten days or so, and D. B. Low
With specialistic suavity
Soon searches out, beyond a doubt,
The echo of a cavity.

> Ten days or so, and so, and so;
> I find my thoughts' depravity
> Begin to hint there is small stint
> Of treasure in this cavity.

It would seem to prove how empty I had become of creative vigour when I could cease at once from versifying without any regret. It was also a suitable moment with regard to the quantity of verse which I had written during the past three years; the quality was beginning to deteriorate as the making tended to become mechanical.

SATURDAY 28
Alex Galloway along: had been greatly impressed by *The Earth Abideth* and went through the book commenting. To hear someone else read one's own verse seems in most instances to give the poetry a quality that one had not assumed before: let us hope that the quality is really brought forth and not a deceptive addition.

SEPTEMBER

WEDNESDAY 1
Got some letters written: how readily a day can be filled by the doing of odd jobs and how easy in circumstances such as mine to drift into the habit of doing only odd jobs which demand no concentration or creative effort. One of the most deplorable aspects of contemporary conditions is that so many are compelled to do 'odd jobs' during the greater part of their life: jobs in which they cannot possibly find the joy of expression.

THURSDAY 2
Writing in the afternoon: a water-wagtail darting about the green; how graceful even with its wagging tail and how lightning-swift in its movement; one could watch the creature for a long time.

MONDAY 6
† The coughing has become more of a nuisance since last I wrote, and about every hour I have to perform a clearing out process which in accumulation wastes a lot of time.

The actual coughing isn't, so far, much of a strain, but my
muscles inserted into the groin region have become strained
and any sudden cough produces a most painful reaction; this
makes me swear involuntarily. Fortunately, as yet, my sleep
is little disturbed; and I am wakened but once or twice by
the need to get rid of phlegm. One accepts the coughing
as a nuisance, but breathlessness is an aggravation. The
feeling of helplessness and frustration during a spell of
breathlessness hurts one's pride and one grows angry. In
our temporary weakness we tend to become childish; and
not a few times my face has automatically puckered up as if
I were about to cry: in the humiliation of extreme weakness
one might actually cry like a child.

† The curse of a cough is not that it curtails one's speech
only but also one's laughter; the involuntary expression of
mirth becomes guarded, and full enjoyment is modified.
This condition would seem to react upon the feelings, and
one begins to note fewer occasions for laughter: it is in one's
sense of humour as a gradual diminution of memory.

WEDNESDAY 8
Glad to learn that proofs of *Seeds in the Wind* 5 will be ready
at the end of the week: how much fun, one sometimes feels,
might have been given to Scottish children by these rhymes
if our language had been wholly active and alive. I cannot
keep down the presumptuous thought that I am a better
writer of verse for bairns than Stevenson, and even De la
Mare—but there are so few to listen.

† In July I took the thought to note down the gifts
which kindly folk bring, and at the end of the month
I was astonished at all that had been given to me; such
generosity is well-nigh incredible. July is a record month,
yet August was almost as rich in gifts.

SUNDAY 12
† To-day after my ablutions, which are now a real strain
on me due to my turning—or rather pulling myself—from
side to side, I had got flatter down on the bed and when I
tried to push myself up and over on to my left side so that
Mops could remove the bolster I was unable to do so: after
a little by altering my position I was able to raise myself.

But the incident definitely proved that I had weakened a fair amount lately; and this knowledge together with breathlessness made me quite irritable for a bit. I really must try to control these irritable exhibitions which have been on the increase lately—lot of pride to be knocked out of me yet.

SATURDAY 18

On looking out on to the green at this moment I saw a starling approach a sparrow which had a bit of bread; merely by a hostile gesture the sparrow made the starling clear off; on its returning a little later the starling was again sent packing by the same gesture. Rather surprising when as a tribe the starlings are a squabbling lot. . . . Reading: I read practically nothing now; and like these two other 'pleasures of life' which I have forsworn—the making of verse and smoking—I am in no way fretted by the deprivation. This would suggest that either my sensitivity has grown dull, or that I have fully learned the teaching of necessity.

† I fancy I noted somewhere lately that an obvious sign of my increasing weakness was the satisfaction which I found at the end of the day in the thought that I would soon be asleep. This anticipation is not wholly explained by tiredness or restlessness but has an element in it however small, of the desire for a period of complete stillness and forgetfulness; a thought which can hardly be explained otherwise than deathwardly: we wish to return to our earthly silence. And even from the very qualified urgency of this wish we can appreciate the welcome which the severe sufferer gives to the moment which brings his narcotic, and of the ultimate cry of the whole being for oblivion. The desire is wholly human, and most natural as it originates in the body and is a cry from the flesh rather than the mind: it is not calculating but causal. So long as the senses can appreciate the world with a modicum of gladness, so long the wish to live remains, if the mind is not unbalanced; but when pain has grown so strong that the mind and senses are withdrawn from outward contemplation into a core of mere endurance, then the mind through the misery of sense asks

the question: *If the world is now a nothingness let us pass away from it?*

SUNDAY 19

† Now that breathlessness makes me unwilling to exert myself physically I also find that there is a parallel tendency in the mind to take things easy. To indulge this laziness to any extent would be fatal, as with general weakness such an easing of will-power would increase rapidly; and it is only by regularity of application that I can have a hope of rounding off the various odd-jobs which I wish to see completed. It is, in genial circumstances such as mine, easy to forget the urgency that is about one, and especially so when one does not brood. Accordingly, it is perhaps not altogether a bad thing to be jostled into concern about the duration of one's life by a symptom of increasing mortality. A jab from death's elbow to remind one that he is still under the obligations of life.

TUESDAY 21

† This morning about 8.30 I had a most disturbing experience. I began to cough, and a lot of phlegm gathered. I kept on coughing but could dislodge nothing, and after I was pretty well exhausted I found that my windpipe seemed nearly blocked. I began again to cough again but to no purpose—the matter merely coming up so far and then going back again. Suddenly I felt I was choking, and for a while a spasmodic coughing and gasping for breath went on with the continued up and down shifting of the phlegm. Just when I thought I was to be deprived of breath altogether a slight passage was cleared and I was able to rest: by now my heart was pounding fiercely, and it was a good while later before I was able to clear my throat properly.

† I had not thought of how far I had lapsed from the vitality of youth until I looked on Ian Black yesterday afternoon and had shaken hands with him. Ian certainly looks the part of athletic youth in its prime freshness. He has a mop of bright fair curly hair, his complexion clear and fresh. He is at least 6 ft. 1 in. And solidly built with strong bones but not too large; as he bent over the bed to shake hands I sensed the glowing strength of youth.

WEDNESDAY 22

Just on 2.30, Mrs MacArthur[6] came in carrying a bunch
of flowers. She proved to be a pleasant woman and smart
in her movements. In her busy life on a hill-farm her
dominating thoughts are about her poetry; and considering
the many troubles she has had to face it is well she had
this preoccupation. She brought photographs of her three
boys—two of whom have died during the war. The eldest,
and no doubt her greatest pride, a very frank-looking
and handsome lad: after an hour and a half's talking
Mrs MacArthur said cheerio at 4.0, leaving me a copy
of Drinan's *The Men of the Rocks*.[7]

SUNDAY 26

† I wonder if breathlessness reduces one to childish behaviour more readily than other forms of weakness. To-day,
when my pillows at the weekly bed-changing required
far more readjustment than usual, I displayed a peevishness which in retrospect was most humiliating. It seemed
incredible that a man of my age should act like a bairn
and be brought by frustration to the verge of tears. I must
be weaker than I know, surely; and as weak in will as in
body—for there is no indication yet of this increasing stoic
calm that I imagined I would gradually achieve.

† I hope I shall be remembered as a poet, if for no other
reason than that my folks may not be forgotten, nor the
fact that they had done so much for me and had received
so little in return.

MONDAY 27

† It was somewhat ironical listening to Jim's repetition from
his letter last night—that now I could rest from writing
concentrated verse with its roots in the problems of to-day,
and plunge into a sea of coloured words revelling there as I
splashed out shapes and music and rich scenes. Jim becomes
so enthusiastic that one almost feels sorry to disappoint him.
Just before Jim left, Tilly and Bernard Smith came in. What
a contrast in natures: Jim with his vast general knowledge,
his absorption in the restitution of Thomas Duncan, his
many interests outside his own particular sphere. And Tilly

and Bernard model citizens in their own way, and yet but partially alive, having no vital contact with the world of 'mortal' immortality where one learns the wisdom, and looks up [to] the glory, of life. But such as do not become heirs of this kingdom are [un]aware of what they have lost; they are according[ly] able to grow well-content with the little circle of their world: are they not secure, in comfort, blessed with bonnie bairns, sure of good faring and friends like themselves. What might not have happened to them if with imagination clear-eyed they had gazed into some abyss of the human spirit with Dostoievsky; if they had learned something of Tolstoy's magnanimity or had a glimpse of the great humanity of Shakespeare or Balzac? Who would care to assume the responsibility of startling them out of their parish in which they work and take their ease in self-satisfied mediocrity. Has any the right to do so but life?

† Had palpitation a few times last night, and noted that although the blood went quickly about the body it gave me the sensation that it had to use extra force to pass through the heart, as if it had thickened in some way and got partially hindered there.

TUESDAY 28

It gave one rather a startled feeling when the other day, having noted down the hope that I might be remembered as a poet, Jim Finlayson produced a short notice of *But the Earth Abideth* in which I am referred to as 'probably the greatest living Scottish poet': nonsense, of course, so long as MacDiarmid breathes. If it were true—what a queer position for a leading poet—to have been sending out poetry for 20 years, and still compelled to issue it in book form at his own expense. And as regards his verse in English—to remain after 20 years almost wholly unknown so that, apart from exception, he has appeared in none of the anthologies published during that lengthy period:[8] we had better gang canniely.

WEDNESDAY 29

There is a quirkiness about a diary which cannot be assessed: something which may seem to the diarist himself to be of real importance may in later days prove a bore;

and some little aside or comment which just dropped from his pen, by the way, may prove to be a most penetrating glimpse of a situation, or a revelationary flash lighting up some strange corner of the spirit. The true diary is one, therefore, in which the diarist is, in the main, communing with himself, conversing openly and without pose so that trifles will not be absent, nor the intimate little confessions and resolutions which if voiced at all must be voiced in such a private confessional as this.

† How circumstance alters the importance of a thing. To-day I started my potato and vegetable dish in place of meat and it was astonishing how I enjoyed the meal. I can say truly that for a very long time now I have not been given so much pleasure as I had to-day from two potatoes unmashed, a piece of cooked turnip, and three or four sections of carrot. It was delicious to taste the true flavour of the potato not contaminated in the least by the touch of gravy or grease. It is this joy of having things in their native purity that seems to give me great satisfaction now. Can it be not merely a somatic liking prompted in some way by my trouble but also a psychological desire. Now that my own body must become an increasing object of corruption I would have at least only uncontaminated food entering it; perhaps with a vague notion that the purity might react on the rottenness within.

OCTOBER

MONDAY 4

Writing in the forenoon. Sometimes one is deceived when a smallish and light-coloured leaf slants from the syca-more—was that a leaf or are the yorlins still darting about the tree? . . . Writing in the afternoon: it is ironic to recall these numerous, too numerous, entries in my diary asserting that one must keep the senses keen and alert—and now by dozing I would seem to lose a quarter of the 'working' day! It appears as if a good lot of toxin is now formed in the bloodstream. . . . Sheena Mitchell came in to talk over some of her 'Highers' subjects. A very intelligent girl. . . . Sheena got a few books which might help her a bit.

WEDNESDAY 6

How snail-like the tempo at which I seem to be living now—and yet my days are hurrying out of the world. I do not think any of my friends suspect as yet that I am under the sentence of death; and it will be fine if they continue for a good while yet to imagine that I have a touch of bronchitis or something like that: when at last they know, an undefinable restraint will come between the free interchanges of friendship.

† Desire, if one may use so strong a word, has been completely transferred from the thought of women to considerations of 'what we shall eat, and what we shall drink'. The other evening it came to me almost as a relief that for many months the attractiveness of women no longer disturbed me; that neither in dream or day-dream was I fretted by images of passion. Everything in my life is being quieted; and the great orbit of life is moving in from the bounds of the universe like the gradually diminishing circle of light from a wasting flame. Whether the mood adapts itself to the changing environment, or whether I have somehow achieved a sense of proportion which adapts itself readily to the inevitable, I am scarcely touched by regret or anxiety; but derive even an element of satisfaction from being able to stand back and watch myself busied or idling under the shadow of a doom which is but rarely remembered. So much can wither away from the human spirit and yet the great gift of the ordinary day remains: the stability of the small things of life which yet in their constancy are the greatest. All the daily kindness; the little obligations, the signs of remembrance in the homely gifts: these do not pass, but still hearten the body and spirit to the verge of the grave.

THURSDAY 7

† I find that quite unconsciously—and seemingly incongruously—I am personifying parts of myself, clothing, etc. The end of my undervest for example is American—probably a young millionaire who is rather careless about himself.

Sometimes there are little pieces of loose skin on my under-lip, inside a little way: these I consider horses on a plain. In certain positions the ridge of my spine near the waist is pressed directly by the compressed pillow and I have hurriedly to knuckle a hollow for the bones. I think of the bones here as a set of rather shoddy young fellows who have a tendency to act vindictively.

FRIDAY 8

† I wonder if the weariness, an intensifying condition in myself, is caused quite as much by the environment of war as by the bodily factors operating in myself. Daily we are bombarded by the reports, all similar in kind, of bombings, shellings, minings, blastings. sinkings, burnings; daily we meet someone who repeats what newspaper and radio have already told us: daily we see food of the same unappetising quality appear on the table (unless when one is lucky to get some home-made fare). Our body and soul cry out for change and refreshment; for the expansiveness of a world untrammelled by excessive regulation. We want to feel that earth has been washed clean again, and that from her comes the uncontaminated richness of fruit and grain. A few simple things could bring about change, a sense of freedom, and the return of the joy in earth. And if such a one placed in a privileged position can have so intense longings—what agonies of desire must be experienced by the millions of destitute folk on the continent.

SATURDAY 9

Three starlings alighted on the ridge of the oak-fence between the two gardens: two of them were so light in colour that one would maintain they were youngsters: probably a late brood.

SUNDAY 10

Phone message from J. B. Salmond9 saying he'd be up in the afternoon if suitable. . . . J. B. and Mrs Salmond stepped in about 2.0—came up by bus: Salmond seems to have quite recovered from his bad time; thinner but he could stand some thinning: jawed on until about 4.0 when Douglas Young stalked in—looking fresh: up to talk at some I.L.P. meeting. All friends off at 4.0 or so: thought it a very kindly thing that J. B. should come up specially to see me and enquire about my health.

TUESDAY 12

† Yesterday's experience of coughing for 3 hours without clearance . . . was a most wearing one and left me very limp indeed. . . . From this incident I can guess that many very unpleasant experiences are awaiting me; and one of the most unfortunate consequences is the loss of time. The breathing remains exceptionally shallow, and one has to make an effort with some care to avoid bodily inconvenience. How quickly one may be brought down by this sort of strain is seen in my temporal hollows which have slightly deepened in the past two days. Of course, all the abdominal muscles are on a strain and tend to remain so for a while, affecting appetite in a negative way. To-day I have been controlling my coughing with care whenever possible. Phlegm continues to be watery, but the sweetish smell is less apparent. However, if one is not clearing one must be collecting more and more: it is not a satisfying choice either way.

WEDNESDAY 13

Writing in the forenoon: G. G., with the concern of an elder brother, trotted in to find if I was more settled this morning: I could say that I was, but that that was due in the main to the fact that I wasn't attempting to get rid of the phlegm. The stuff was accordingly accumulating—and could not but be a factor in the increase of breathlessness and palpitation: thus one is threatened from all around, by night and by day: whichever way one may turn the net is closing and cannot be evaded.

THURSDAY 14

† One or two odd points to be noted. During spells of drowsiness I find that I am now gaining a certain amount of satisfaction by speaking out a sentence now and then in a deep voice. Often these have no relation to anything; but many times they are prompted by the imagery that may be passing over my almost dreaming mind. Some incident takes place and I ask a question about it as if the folks

knew my thoughts. I imagine if deeply enough drowsed that someone is in the room; and when I get no answer to my query I am always surprised that I have not been heard: usually I open my eyes and realise that I have been half-asleep. This forenoon, however, just after my bed had been made and while mother was dusting, I suddenly fell into a doze, and heard a vivid account by Jean Soutar of an accident to two soldiers just at Fran's cottage. When Jean had finished I asked Mops if she had heard how the soldiers were getting on. She was quite mystified—and I had to explain the matter. Last night I must have been talking quite a lot; as the folks said they heard me making noises round about 1.30.

Notes

CHAPTER ONE. 1930

1. William Soutar's doctor. They were old friends, school-boys together at Perth Academy and fellow-students at Edinburgh University.
2. Sir (then Mr) John Fraser, the specialist whom Soutar had first consulted in 1923.
3. Soutar's cousin.
4. The adopted daughter of Soutar's parents.

CHAPTER TWO. 1931

1. See *Poems in Scots* (The Moray Press, Edinburgh, 1935).

CHAPTER THREE. 1932

1. See *Seeds in the Wind* (The Moray Press, Edinburgh, 1933; revised and enlarged edition, Andrew Dakers, London, 1943; illustrated edition, Dakers, 1948).
2. 'Hugh MacDiarmid' (Christopher Murray Grieve, 1892–1978), poet, critic and journalist. Publications include (verse) *Sangschaw* (1925), *A Drunk Man Looks at the Thistle* (1926), *Stony Limits* (1934), & *Collected Poems* (1962), *The Complete Poems* (1978); (prose) *Annals of the Five Senses* (1923), *Contemporary Scottish Studies* (1926), *Scottish Eccentrics* (1936), *Lucky Poet* (1943). Editor of *The Collected Poems of William Soutar* (Dakers, London, 1948).
3. William Montgomerie, b.1904, poet and editor. Author of *Via* (1933), *Squared Circle* (1934), *From Time to Time* (1985); editor (with Norah Montgomerie) of *Scottish Nursery Rhymes* (1946); (1985), *Sandy Candy* (1948), *The Well at the World's End* (1956).
4. Soutar's cousin ('Toke').
5. Two of Soutar's oldest friends, his schoolfellows at Perth Academy. William Mackenzie, Soutar's cousin,

had written freelance journalism. James Finlayson was a painter, and after Soutar's death his portrait of the poet hung in the latter's room in his house in Perth.

CHAPTER FOUR. 1933

1. Neil M. Gunn (1891–1973), novelist, dramatist and essayist. Publications include *Morning Tide* (1931), *Sun Circle* (1933), *The Silver Darlings* (1941), *Young Art and Old Hector* (1942), *The Green Isle of the Great Deep* (1944), *The Drinking Well* (1946), *The Well at the World's End* (1951), *The Other Landscape* (1954).

2. C. J. Jung, *Psychology of the Unconscious* (2nd impression, 1922), p.226.

3. *Collected Poems* (1948), p.280

4. *Poems of William Soutar*, ed. W. R. Aitken (Scottish Academic Press, Edinmburgh, 1988), p.209. For 3 and 4 see also Jung, *op. cit.*, p. 156.

5. William Jeffrey (1894–1946), poet and critic. Publications include *The Wise Men Come to Town* (1923), *Mountain Songs* (1928), *Eagle of Coruisk* (1933), *Fantasia Written in an Industrial Town* (1933), *Sea Glimmer* (1947); *Selected Poems*, edited by Alexander Scott (Serif Books, Edinburgh, 1951). At the time of this meeting, Jeffrey was on the staff of *The Glasgow Herald*.

6. William Power (1873–1951), critic and journalist. Editor of *The Scots Observer* (1926–29).

7. James Whyte was at this time editor of *The Modern Scot*.

8. Francis George Scott (1880–1958), composer. Publications include *Scottish Lyrics* (6 vols.). Scott was C. M. Grieve's teacher while 'Hugh MacDiarmid' was at school in Langholm, Dumfriesshire, and many of Scott's songs are settings of poems by his erstwhile pupil.

9. Chapman and Hall, London, 1931.

10. *Collected Poems* p.259.

CHAPTER FIVE. 1934

1. The Moray Press, Edinburgh, 1934.

CHAPTER SIX. 1935

1. 'Lewis Grassic Gibbon' (J. Leslie Mitchell, 1901–1935), novelist and essayist. Publications include *Sunset Song* (1932), *Cloud Howe* (1933), *Grey Granite* (1934)—issued together as the trilogy *A Scots Quair* (1946)—and, with Hugh MacDiarmid, *Scottish Scene* (1934).

2. The Moray Press, Edinburgh, 1935. One hundred epigrams.

3. Jarrolds, London, 1932. The first volume of the trilogy *A Scots Quair*.

4. See 'Autobiography' (entry in Soutar's diary for 12th July, 1937).

CHAPTER SEVEN. 1936

1. Jarrolds, London, 1934. The third volume of Gibbon's trilogy.

2. See 'Cadger Jimmy' (entry in Soutar's diary for 25th May, 1942).

3. See 'Tricks o' the Trade', *Poems*, p.158.

CHAPTER EIGHT. 1937

1. Christopher Murray Grieve ('Hugh MacDiarmid').

2. This book was advertised for the 'Voice of Scotland' series published by Routledge, London, but did not appear.

3. See entry in Soutar's diary for 20th November, 1935.

4. See 'The Proposal' (entry in Soutar's diary for 21st February, 1942).

CHAPTER NINE. 1938

1. Oxford University Press, 2nd impression, 1926. Soutar frequently contributed to *The Adelphi* during Murry's editorship of that magazine.

2. See 'Second Childhood', *Poems*, p.163.

3. See 'The Children', *Poems*, p.26.

4. Soutar's opinion of Messrs. Chamberlain, Daladier, Hitler, and Mussolini at Munich is pungently expressed in an unpublished poem from a notebook, entitled 'A Mess of Plottage'.

There were four cooks, ho! very fine cooks,
Who met to make a plot:
Adolph and Musso and La-deeda
And the Flying Chamberpot.

Wind and lies, wind and lies,
And a mesmerising smell,
They muddled and mixed; muddled and mixed;
Muddled and mixed them well.

They brought their plottage to the boil
And opened the windows wide:
They laughed to see the fumy cloud
Roll over the country-side.

Wind and lies . . . etc.

Some folks sniffed death upon the wind,
Some folks were choked with lies:
But most of the folk snuffed up the smell—
The smell that can mesmerise.

Wind and lies . . . etc.

CHAPTER TEN. 1939

1. Soutar and his friend James Finlayson had had a disagreement on Scottish Nationalist politics.

2. See *Riddles in Scots* (The Moray Press, Edinburgh, 1937).

CHAPTER ELEVEN. 1940

1. Tom Scott, b.1917, poet and controversialist. Author of *Brand the Builder* (1975), etc.

2. G. S. Fraser (1915–1979), poet and scholar. Publications include *Home Town Elegy* (1944), *The Traveller Has Regrets* (1948), *The Modern Writer and His World* (1953), *Poems* (1981). Fraser, with Tom Scott, had visited Soutar on an earlier occasion.

3. Alex Galloway, b.1908. Author of *War Poems in Scots* (1942).

4. Douglas Young, (1913–1973), poet and scholar.

Publications include *Auntran Blads* (1943), *A Braird o' Thristles* (1947), *Chasing an Ancient Greek* (1950).

CHAPTER TWELVE. 1941

1. George Bruce, b.1909, poet and critic. Author of *Sea Talk* (1943), *Selected Poems* (1947), *Landscape and Figures* (1967), *Collected Poems* (1971), *Perspectives* (1987).

2. See Hugh MacDiarmid's lines—

> The Rose of all the world is not for me.
> I want for my part
> Only the little white rose of
>   Scotland
> That smells sharp and sweet
> —and breaks the heart.

3. James Finlayson.

4. 'A sympathetic composer, and friend of Soutar's, like Mr Francis George Scott, has only been able to set two or three of his pieces'. Hugh MacDiarmid, *Collected Poems of William Soutar*, 'Introduction', p.17.

CHAPTER THIRTEEN. 1942

1. See entry in Soutar's diary for 15th July, 1937.

2. See entry in Soutar's diary for 29th June, 1936.

CHAPTER FOURTEEN. 1943

1. Douglas Young had been imprisoned as a result of upholding his contention that, according to the Act of Union of 1707, the British Parliament had no right to conscript Scottish citizens.

2. These lines are written in the margin of 'Epitaph'—as if, to Soutar the poet, the prospect of his own death was of less importance than the death of the mythical Johnnie.

3. Sydney Goodsir Smith (1915–1975), poet, critic, dramatist, novelist. At this time Soutar had seen only Smith's first collection, *Skail Wind* (1941), which Soutar thought 'a queer book'. Other publications include *Under the Eildon Tree* (1948) and *So Late into the Night* (1952).

4.   Dakers, London, 1943.

5.   The second (revised and enlarged) edition was pub-
      lished by Dakers, London, 1943, after Soutar's death.

6.   Bessie J. B. Macarthur (1889–c.1975), poet. Author of
      Scots Poems (1938), *Last Leave* (1943), *From Daer
      Water* (1962).

7.   'Adam Drinan' (Joseph Macleod), *The Men of the
      Rocks* (The Fortune Press, London [1942].

8.   Since Soutar's death, his poems in English (as well as
      in Scots) have appeared in the following anthologies—
      Poems of Our Time, chosen by Richard Church and
      M. M. Bozman (Everyman's Library, Dent, London,
      1945); *Modern Scottish Poetry*, edited by Maurice
      Lindsay (Faber, London, 1946, 1966; Carcanet Press,
      Manchester, 1976; Robert Hale, London 1986); *The
      Oxford Book of Scottish Verse*, edited by John MacQueen
      and Tom Scott (Clarendon Press, Oxford, 1966);
      Twelve Modern Scottish Poets, edited by Charles King
      (University of London Press, London, 1971); *Voices
      of Our Kind*, edited by Alexander Scott (Chambers,
      Edinburgh, 1987).

9.   At this time Salmond was editor of *The Scots
      Magazine*.

Index of Names